THE
MODERN READER'S
GUIDE TO ACTS

THE
MODERN READER'S
GUIDE TO ACTS

ALBERT E. BARNETT

ASSOCIATION PRESS · NEW YORK

The Modern Reader's Guide to Acts

Copyright © 1962 by
National Board of Young Men's Christian Associations

Association Press, 291 Broadway, New York 7, N.Y.

Price, 50 cents

Publisher's stock number: 549

Library of Congress catalog card number: 62-9380

Printed in the United States of America

To THEODORE HENLEY JACK, who as
my college teacher of history first
aroused in me a taste for careful
scholarship by his own exemplifica-
tion of it.

PREFACE

This *Guide* undertakes to facilitate the modern reader's comprehension of the account of Christian beginnings presented in The Acts of the Apostles. Such assistance in understanding any ancient writing is necessary. That necessity is immeasurably increased in the case of biblical books, because people expect to find in the Bible practical guidance for twentieth-century living.

The *Guide* will not take the place of firsthand acquaintance with Acts. It will accomplish its purpose in making intelligible what the author meant when he wrote for Theophilus and the generation he typified.

Within the limits imposed by space, the *Guide* will attempt to clarify the logic of Luke's narrative, what the stories included in the narrative tell about the early Church, how these stories refute misrepresentation, and the exposition of the gospel they lay before readers.

The citations and references to the Bible herein are from the Revised Standard Version of The Holy Bible.

CONTENTS

INTRODUCTION

The Acts of the Apostles is clearly the second half of a two-volume account of Christian beginnings. The first volume tells the story of what Jesus "began to do and teach." The second narrates what Jesus as head of the Church continues "to do and teach" through the Spirit.

The two halves of this monumental work became separated in the first quarter of the second century. At that time, the Four Gospels were published as four versions of *The Gospel*. Overlooking the indissoluble unity of Gospel and Acts, the second-century editor who gave the Church the fourfold Gospel left Acts isolated. He might better have included it in a fivefold Gospel. It is in fact a fifth gospel.

In the course of the canonization of the New Testament, Acts ceased to be known as *The Acts of the Living Christ* and became mistakenly entitled *The Acts of the Apostles*. Under that title, it became an introduction to the epistles of the apostles: James; First and Second Peter; First, Second, and Third John; and Jude. It so stands today in The New Testament in Greek. The understanding of Luke and Acts suffered by their separation. Each sheds light on the other, for the total of their meaning is greater than the sum of the parts.

One author wrote both halves of this earliest account of Christian beginnings. The prefaces of the two books clearly make Acts the sequel to Luke. The story is merely begun in the gospel. Many details illustrate this. The prospect in Luke 9:51 of Jesus' being "received up" is completed in the account of his Ascension in Acts 1:9-11. The promise that believers will be "clothed with power from on high" in Luke 24:49 is fulfilled by the bestowal of the Spirit at Pentecost (Acts 2:1-4).

That the author was Luke is implied in the relevant New Testament allusions. According to Colossians 4:14 and Philemon 24, Luke was Paul's companion during his Roman imprisonment. The use of the first person plural in Acts 16:10-18, 20:5-16, 21:1-18, and 27:1-28 suggests the incorporation of a travel diary in Acts. The keeper of that diary was with Paul in Macedonia, traveled with him to Syria, and accompanied him to Rome. If the diarist was also the author of Luke-Acts, he was more probably Luke than any other known associate of Paul. That the author of Acts shows no acquaintance with Paul's letters does not lower this probability. It means merely that Paul's letters were yet unpublished and that the author knew the apostle personally instead of through the medium of his letters.

Interestingly, the travel diary centers around Philippi. Except for the journey to Rome, the "We" sections locate Paul and his company in the vicinity of that Macedonian city. The author designates it as "the leading city . . . of Macedonia," more nearly a reflection of understandable pride in his home town than of historical accuracy. That Luke first met Paul at Troas and urged him to visit Macedonia may well have been the background of the vision in which "a man of Macedonia was standing beseeching him . . . 'Come over . . . and help us' " (Acts 16:12). More frequently than by the spectacular and miraculous, God speaks to men through normal media of this sort.

Acts was written at Ephesus in the last decade of the first century. It thus belonged to the same climate of circumstances as Ephesians, Revelation, the Gospel of John, Hebrews, and First Peter. The Church was suspected of sedition by the imperial government. The Roman historian Tacitus tells of emerging governmental hostility under Nero (*Annals* xv. 44). Pliny tells of the extension of that hostility from Rome to the provinces (*Letters* x. 96-97; *Natural History* iv.

12,23). The five New Testament books mentioned shared the common purpose to encourage the Church in frightening times and to refute slanderous reports based on misinformation.

Theophilus and his generation and/or class typified Luke's audience. Identification of Theophilus is important, but inconclusive. He could have been a recent convert, who, like third- and fourth-generation Christians, generally needed to know how the Church which began humbly in Palestine had now by Divine Providence established itself in all principal cities of the Empire.

The English word "catechumen," meaning a new convert, is derived from the Greek verb used in Luke 1:4, where the evangelist thinks that Theophilus needs accurate instruction. That verb describes the instruction of new converts in Acts 18:25.

Preponderantly, however, the evidence suggests that Theophilus was a Roman provincial official, whose misinformation about the Church lay at the root of governmental hostility. The salutation "Most Excellent" in Luke 1:3 is used of Felix in Acts 23:26 and 24:3, and of Festus in Acts 26:25. Furthermore, the verb used in Acts 18:25 regarding new converts describes false information given by enemies against Paul in Acts 21:21,24. Finally, the verb in Luke 1:4 describing the desire that Theophilus "may know the truth" is precisely the verb used in Acts 21:34 and 22:30 describing official investigation by a Roman military commander.

Luke assumes that Christian history is the gospel's most persuasive resource for evangelism and defense. The Christian facts arouse and support faith. They also warn misinformed enemies of the Church that they may place themselves in the hazardous position of "opposing God" (Acts 5:39; cf. Heb. 2:2f.; 4:12f.; 10:26-31).

Entirely apart from the conscious intention of the author, Acts inspired a venture in publication the cumulative outcome of which was the New Testament. The impressive account it gave of the personality and service of Paul inspired an unidentified leader in the Asian Church, conceivably Onesimus, to collect and publish Paul's letters. Already possessing Colossians and Philemon, he used the account of Paul's journeys in Acts as a sort of road map to retrace the apostle's steps and obtain copies of his extant letters. These letters, previously in local hands and lacking any general circulation, were by this means given to the Church as a published collection between 95 and 100 A.D. By that means, Paul was enabled again to speak to the Church during the troubled times in which Acts, Ephesians, the Fourth Gospel, Hebrews, Revelation, and First

Peter appeared. Their usefulness ultimately brought about their canonization.

In 144 A.D., Marcion, a Christian scholar at Rome, proposed that Christian Scriptures take the place of the Old Testament, which he regarded as the Scriptures of the Synagogue. The canon Marcion proposed consisted of Luke's gospel and the published letters of Paul. After Marcion, every version of the New Testament contained this original ten-letter corpus of Paul's letters. That collection was the nucleus of the larger body of writings that became the New Testament during the third and fourth centuries of the Christian era.

Speeches amount to a fifth of the total length of Acts. They explain the meaning of the events that make up the narrative. They serve also to relieve the monotony of an otherwise unbroken and not too evidently correlated story of Christian beginnings. A special introductory word about these speeches is essential in any adequate guide for the modern reader. The principal speeches of Christian participants in Luke's narrative are:

Peter   1:16-22;   2:14-36;   3:12-26;   4:8-12;
           10:34-43; 11:5-17; 15:7-11
James   15:14-21; 21:20-25
Stephen 7:2-53

Paul   13:16-41; 14:15-17; 17:22-31; 20:18-
        35; 22:1, 3-21; 23:1,6; 24:10-21; 26:2-
        23; 28: 17-20

Speeches by non-Christian participants in the
narrative are:

Gamaliel 5:35-39
The Ephesian Town Clerk 19:35-39
Tertullus 24:2-8
Festus 25:14-21,24-27

In this use of speeches by actors in his narrative, Luke employed a literary device widely current in antiquity for the creation of verisimili-
tude. It mattered little whether the speeches
were absolutely historical verbatim or the formulation by the writer according to his understanding of what must have been said. Those of the
latter type would be thoroughly historical in
the sense of disclosing issues currently real for
the author's own situation. That the speeches in
their present (Lukan) formulation were not the
exact words of the original speakers detracts
nothing from the reliability of the narrative in
which they were set. That such is the character
of the speeches in Acts seems highly probable
for the reasons now to be given.

A careful reading of the Greek text leaves little doubt that the language and style of the
speeches are identical with those of the book as

a whole. The voice is Luke's, even if it be held
that the substance belongs to Peter, Stephen,
James, and Paul. Language and style point to a
single authorship. This is much more impressively
true of the speeches in Acts than when Luke
incorporates materials from such identifiable
written sources such as Mark and "Q" in his first
volume.

Again, the occasions that evoked these speeches
are of a character that imply no written account
of what was said. Nor do they allow for any
assumption of note-taking by auditors. Also logi-
cally unlikely would be the supposition that the
speakers subsequently repeated for disciples
what had been said in the original instance. The
circumstances per se all but preclude the de-
velopment of an oral tradition of the apostolic
speeches reported in Acts.

Despite the difficulties, those who feel that
primitive preaching is dependably summarized
in the speeches of Acts point to the record of
Jesus' words in Luke's gospel as a convincing
parallel. They contend that if the speeches in
Acts are entirely Lukan the speeches in the gospel half of the two-volume publication must also
be. That, however, is a complete *non sequitur!*
Abundant evidence supports the currency of a
fairly fixed oral tradition of Jesus' words, later
incorporated in the written Greek sources ab-

sorbed in the Synoptic Gospels. But no such evidence exists for the speeches in Acts.

Such evidence as does exist decisively refutes the assumption that the speeches in Acts rest upon a tradition of primitive apostolic preaching. Papias of Hierapolis, writing in about 125 A.D., explicitly says that Peter's preaching supplied Mark with the substance of his gospel (Eusebius *Church History* iii. 39. 5-7). For acquaintance with Peter's preaching, then, one will refer to Mark's gospel, not the speeches in Acts. The speeches of Paul in Acts, similarly, agree so poorly with those found in the apostle's letters as to make improbable a preservation in Acts of an independent oral tradition of his preaching.

Logical improbability in the matter is also so great as itself to constitute negative evidence. Regarding Jesus as they did, the establishment of a tradition of his words and deeds was natural for his followers. On the basis of great memories and ardent expectations, the earliest Christians ordered their lives, solved their problems, determined the content of their preaching. But the apostles and their immediate followers, in possession of the tradition of Jesus' words and deeds, lacked the incentive to create a parallel tradition. Nor were they held in the kind of reverence that would suggest such a tradition in primitive times. Idealization of the apostles begins to take form

during the closing decade of the first century in
references to Christ's "holy apostles" as "foundations . . . of the household of God" (Eph. 2:19;
3:6; Rev. 21:14-21). Paul surely did not so think
of them (Gal. 1:17-20; 2:1-10; I Cor. 3:1-14). Nor
did they so regard each other. The speeches of
Acts are themselves a part of this idealizing tend-
ency and are thus a fundamental element in a
book belonging to the decade in which Ephesians, Revelation, Hebrews, and First Peter originated.

The real parallel to the speeches of Acts is
found in the equally prominent discourses of the
Fourth Gospel. By common consent, those discourses are taken to be formulations of the theology of the Evangelist. They are rarely taken
into account in a study of Jesus' own message.
Precisely that is the soundest view of the
speeches in Acts. They represent what Luke
thought the leaders of an earlier time might have
said. For an intermediate period, this gives these
speeches the kind of relevance to the preaching
of the early Church that the Apostles' Creed,
formulated around 150 A.D. for the refutation of
gnosticism, possesses.

1

DIVINE PURPOSE
EXPLAINS THE CHURCH

ACTS 1:1 TO 2:47

Jesus and the Church (Acts 1:1-5). That Jesus founded the Church and remains its Living Head is the confident faith of Acts 1:1 to 2:47. This conviction is specifically expressed in 1:1-5.

Implicit in this introductory paragraph is the representation that the Church existed germinally in the fellowship of Jesus and his disciples. Matthew specifically and formally makes Jesus the Church's founder (16:18). More indirectly, Luke makes the Church a continuation of collaboration with Jesus by recounting that Judas' successor would necessarily be a man who had "accompanied" the disciples "during all the time that the Lord Jesus went in and out" among them, "from the baptism of John until the day when he was taken up." This would make him also "a witness to his resurrection" (Acts 1:22).

Jesus created the dynamic impetus for the Church and continued to be its Lord and Guide. Just as the Resurrection confirmed the Church's

faith in Jesus' messiahship, Pentecost actualized
his presence in its midst. Thus, instead of being
eclipsed in the "resurrection faith" of the Church,
the authority of Jesus' example and message was
greatly enhanced.

As founder and continuing head of the Church,
Jesus guarantees its beneficent character in the
face of false accusation in Domitian's time. Three
times Pontius Pilate had exonerated Jesus. Herod
corroborated that judgment (Luke 23:4,14,22).
Agreement about Jesus made the two Roman
officials lasting friends. Jesus' accusers, by con-
trast, indicted themselves of sedition by asking
the release of Barabbas, "a man who had been
thrown into prison for an insurrection" (Luke
23:19). Thus, from the start, enemies of the
Church were "suspect." Consistently, ever since,
they have opposed God's manifest purposes
(Acts 5:39). Civil authorities in Luke's time
should not be deceived by them.

The Church's Task (Acts 1:6-26). The task of
the Church is "witnessing." The risen Christ had
himself told his followers: "You shall be my witnesses in Jerusalem, and in all Judea and Samaria
and to the end of the earth" (Acts 1:8). Their
fidelity to that commission is displayed in Acts
in the narrative of the stages of Christian expansion: Jerusalem . . . all Judea (Acts 1 to 7);

Samaria (Acts 8 to 12); "the end of the earth" (Acts 13 to 28).

This "witnessing" consisted in illustrating and continuing Jesus' redemptive ministry, not in fomenting sedition, as slanderously charged. In the power of the Holy Spirit, Jesus "went about doing good and healing all that were oppressed by the devil" (Acts 10:38). The same Spirit empowers his "witnesses." Preaching had been Jesus' principal method of action. Inspired preaching continues to be the principal activity of his "witnesses." Peter illustrates this (Acts 1:15ff.; 2:14-47).

Supernatural Empowerment (Acts 2:1-13). Power is capacity to get work done. Jesus' followers, at his direction, waited at Jerusalem for divine empowerment for assuming Jesus' unfinished task of inaugurating the kingdom. Pentecost validated Jesus' promise and signalized his return as the giving of the Holy Spirit to accompany his "witnesses" in their undertaking— which remained also his own. (See Matt. 28:20; Luke 24:13-35; John 14:18-28; II Cor. 3:17f.).

Luke's story of Pentecost is a pictorial account of profound religious experience. Too often its symbolism has obscured the event itself. Experience, of whatever sort—be it said at the outset— is factual, not fanciful. It happens to persons in their adjustment to environment. Persons pass through it, reflect upon its meaning, derive knowledge from its analysis. Experience is in some sense coextensive with consciousness.

With no alteration in basic character, experience varies in type with differing environmental stimuli. Sense experience is the most constant and abundant, and the assumption is that such experience relates the person dependably to his physical surroundings. On any other basis, practical existence would become impossible. More infrequent, but nonetheless real are the moral, social, intellectual, and aesthetic experiences of persons. The artist does not create beauty. Beauty resides in what he sees, and he reports it with greater skill than the casual observer. That this is true makes possible the latter's appreciation of the artist's service. Similarly, the way of the transgressor is "hard" because there is a moral order that takes reprisals against violators with the approximate certainty of the laws of chemistry and physics.

Religious experience has this general character. It is incited by an aspect of the total environment of persons. It is not satisfied nor explained by sensory or social stimuli. Its object of reference lies outside the self, transcends the order of nature, exists beyond society. It consists essentially in the living God inviting man, his creature, into his fellowship and service and in the knowledge of himself that grows out of such fellowship and service.

Experience is never taken exclusively at face value. Invariably, it must be subjected to critical examination. Such examination distinguishes naïvete from scientific knowledge. But experience remains the "raw material" to be investigated and evaluated in the quest for knowledge, whether in physics or metaphysics. Experience in religion no less than experience in general has the character of two-sidedness, and knowledge is the outcome, assuming competent evaluation. This is true of religious experience or it is not true at all!

The New Testament contains three clear references to the religious experience symbolically described in Acts 2:1-4. The three references to the one concrete event are, in chronological order, First Corinthians 15:6 (cf. II Cor. 3:17-18), Acts 2:1-4, and John 20:21-23. Of these, the account in Acts is the most vividly symbolic. In the nature of the case, the symbolism here employed was more intelligible to Luke's first-century readers than to his twentieth-century readers. Because of this, the latter need a "Guide" of the sort here supplied.

The Jewish history and symbolism of Pentecost illuminates its Christian meaning. The day after Passover another feast began, called "The Feast of Unleavened Bread." This day began a

seven-week period for the reaping of barley and
wheat. At the end of this week of weeks (the
fiftieth day) a celebration called Pentecost was
observed (Deut. 16.9; Lev. 23:15,16). Centuries
later it was also the celebration of God's gift of
the Law to Moses at Sinai. Bread to nourish the
body and revelation to guide and discipline the
spirit were the great realities. Both were God's
gifts and emphasized his concern with man's total
life.

Correspondingly, and for Luke providentially,
the day after the seventh Sabbath from Jesus'
resurrection became "Pentecost" for Christians.
The "mighty wind" and the "tongues as of fire"
were familiar biblical symbols of the effective
and purifying presence of the living God (cf.
Exod. 3:2ff.; 13:21f.; Isa. 6:6-8; I Kings 18:38;
19:11-13; Matt. 3:11; 17:2-8; John 3:8).

The biblical analogies of wind and fire are
vivid assertions of the Christian consciousness of
Christ's return with the Holy Spirit. That "witnesses" would serve their risen Lord in world-
wide evangelism is prefigured in the intelligi-
bility of their preaching in the tongue of "every
nation under heaven" (Acts 2:5-13).

Clearly, then, the Church originated, not as
malevolent conspiracy, but as a divinely initi-
ated and empowered fellowship to share the salvation wrought by Jesus Christ with all mankind.

Jesus' earthly example as told in Luke determines what his "witnesses" will be and do. Sacrificial service under his guidance as given by the Spirit establishes the Church's concern and procedure in the world—a far cry from the seditious revolution falsely charged.

The Impact of Peter's Preaching (Acts 2:26-47). Potency takes precedence over ideology in Peter's preaching. Its impact matters most. That was no human achievement. Listeners were "cut to the heart." Their repentance brought forgiveness. Under the Spirit's guidance, they "devoted themselves to the apostles' teaching and fellowship." A new quality of life made the Church heaven's "colony" on earth.

2

DIVINE POWER
AND APOSTOLIC
EFFECTIVENESS

ACTS 3:1 TO 4:31

Compassion and Faith (Acts 3:1-10). In the parable of the Good Samaritan, Jesus correlated compassion with inheritance of eternal life (Luke 10:25-37). A Priest and a Levite, en route home from the Temple, ignored a wounded man by the roadside. But a Samaritan, ineligible to enter the Temple, "had compassion" and extended the practical assistance required by pity.

Luke alone reports that parable. Now he tells how Peter and John, in Jesus' spirit, deal with a handicapped man at the Temple gate. That what happened typified divine action through the apostles is shown by the similar restoration by Paul of "a man . . . who had never walked" (Acts 14:8-11), the one a handicapped Jew, the other a Gentile.

The gate called "Beautiful" opened into the court of the women, the usual place for Jewish worshipers. The third and ninth hours would see throngs passing through that gate (Acts 2:15). Though "laid daily at that gate," the lame man had remained helpless "more than forty years" (Acts 4:22). "Forty" is a biblical symbol of interminability, which in the present case suggested incurability. God's power alone could remedy such a condition.

That the man was forty years old means he was present during Jesus' ministry (Luke 20:1 to 21:38). At the gate where the lame man was daily laid, Jesus had seen "a poor widow put . . . two copper coins" into the treasury and had immortalized her generosity with the comment, "This poor widow has put in more than all of them" (Luke 21:1-4). That the lame man remained for the apostles to heal connects the Church with the ministry of Jesus and shows its character. Jesus came to inaugurate the kingdom of God on earth. He died with that task clarified but not accomplished. The Church began when Jesus' disciples assumed responsibility for his unfinished task. The present story shows that the apostles had learned that "with deeds of love and mercy the heavenly kingdom comes."

Not only so, but the story shows the primacy of life over things and the concern of Christians with man's total life. The lame man asked for money. Instead of merely relieving his mendicancy, the apostles remedied his physical handicap and set him free to make his way in self-respect. "Perfect health" surpassed his fondest expectation (Acts 3:16).

Interestingly, nothing is said about the man's goodness or godliness. As with Jesus, the apostles made the man well before they undertook to make him good (cf. Luke 4:40; 9:2). The sequel to his restoration is that he "entered the Temple" with Peter and John, "walking and leaping and praising God."

The Author of Life (Acts 3:11-26). In distinction from Matthew, where Jesus' message is topically arranged, Luke presents that message in terms of life situations. Consistent with this method, the incident of the lame man's restoration becomes a setting for Peter's sermon (Acts 3:11-26). Redemptive action and inspired preaching complement each other.

The last thing the apostles wanted was notoriety as magicians. Simon and the sons of Sceva learned that with great embarrassment (Acts 8:9-24; 19:14-20). The "power of God unto salvation," not magic, explains what Peter and John do and say. Their "own power and piety," however important, do not account for the paralytic's ability to walk. The truth is that "the God of Abraham and of Isaac and of Jacob . . . glorified his servant Jesus" in giving "perfect health" to the afflicted man. Recovery is complete because God does things that way.

God's power, however, was brought into play by "the faith which is through Jesus" (Acts 3:16). But for the exercise of faith, God's power might never have been individually focused here. Forty years of the man's affliction testify to that. The faith of Peter and John, not the man's faith, brought divine action. The "name" of Jesus stands for the total revelation of God in Christ. Confidence in that revelation and action based on that confidence explain the success of the apostles.

At Capernaum, four friends of an earlier paralytic had removed the roof of Jesus' residence and "let down the pallet" bearing him before the Master. Their faith had invoked Jesus' healing sympathy. Similarly here, the faith of Peter and John brings the paralytic to the "Author of life." Their illustration of what faith can do gives point to their emphasis on faith in their preaching.

In Hebrews 12:2, Jesus arouses faith by being its "pioneer and perfecter." This means that he explored faith in its furthest reaches and pushed its implications to its deepest depths. By playing the role of "pioneer and perfecter" in the present instance, Peter and John show themselves to be true apostles.

Peter's preaching began with exposition. Necessarily, he distinguishes faith from magic. But reproof of sin complements display of truth. Clarification must look toward repentance. "You denied the Holy and Righteous One and asked for a murderer to be granted to you and killed the Author of life" (Acts 3:14f.). That is Peter's indictment. But he proposes, not merciless condemnation, but blessing by "turning everyone . . . from wickedness" (Acts 3:26). Reclamation, not censoriousness, was Peter's motive.

Thus, compassion tinctures accusation. Echoing Jesus' words from the Cross, Peter assures his hearers, "I know that you acted in ignorance as did your rulers" (Acts 3:17; cf. Luke 23:34). The intention of this compassion is to arouse repentance, not excuse from responsibility. For the impenitent, "there remains no longer a sacrifice for sins, but a fearful prospect of judgment, and a fury of fire" which make it indeed "a fearful thing to fall into the hands of the living God" (cf. Heb. 10:26ff.). The Cross in Christian preaching has ever served as an incitement to the grateful faith that saves sinners "from the wrath of God." (Rom. 3:21-26).

The "murderer" preferred to "the Author of life" was clearly Barabbas (cf. Luke 23:18f.). That preference should show where the charge of sedition belonged more properly than at the door of the Church! The Church's Founder and living Head is "the Author of Life," not an incendiary revolutionist (cf. I Pet. 4:15).

The designation of Jesus as "the Author of life" refers immediately to the cure of the paralytic. Beyond that, it means that Jesus inaugurated a reign of grace "through righteousness to eternal life" by his atoning death and victorious resurrection. "The first man was from the earth, a man of dust," said Paul. But "the Second Man is from heaven." This Second Man now functions in the risen Christ as a "life-giving spirit" (I Cor. 15:42-50). In this role, he is presently "the Author of life." His activity explains the "perfect health" of the erstwhile paralytic.

Goodspeed translates Acts 2:24: "For death could not control him." The explanation of death's impotence is that Jesus was and is "the Author of life." Jewish contemporaries, in their ignorance of his true identity, "asked for a murderer." Inadvertently, they served to bring death's impotence to light and opened the way to Christ's timeless return and universal presence as a "life-giving spirit." In Second Timothy the apostle says that "our savior Christ Jesus . . . abolished death and brought life and immortality to light through the gospel" (1:10f.). Of that gospel, Peter feels he is "appointed a preacher and apostle and teacher." By reporting Peter's sermon,

Luke perpetuates the apostolic message that Jesus is timelessly "the Author of life." Luke desires that his readers realize that "the Author of life" is now available and effective for "turning every one from his wickedness" (Acts 3:26).

Enemies of the Apostles (Acts 4:1-12). Slaves of the "high priest" arrested Jesus in Gethsemane. His initial arraignment was before a council composed of "chief priests and scribes" (Luke 22:50). Three times, Pilate, speaking for Rome and corroborated by Herod, exonerated Jesus to those accusers (Luke 23:4ff.). Now the accusers of the Church's Founder secure the arrest of Peter and John (Acts 4:1f.).

The enumeration of the traducers of the apostles makes no mention of the "Herodians" (Acts 4:5f.). Neither in Luke nor in Acts are the Herodians mentioned among opponents of the gospel. They are so designated in Matthew 22:16 and Mark 3:6 and 12:13. Luke's careful avoidance of their mention is part of his defense of the Church against the charge of sedition. Roman authorities throughout Luke-Acts consistently exonerate Christian leaders. Charges against them are regularly thrown out of court as unworthy of governmental notice. Emphasis on the Jewish request for the release of a "murderer" shows where real sedition against Rome was incubated (Acts 3:14; Luke 23:18).

Inspired Boldness (Acts 4:13-31). The "boldness" of Peter and John was more than bravado.
Because "they were filled with the Holy Spirit,"
they "spoke the word of God with boldness"
(Acts 4:13,31). This "boldness" was related to
the "authority" that distinguished Jesus' teaching from that of the scribes (Mark 1:22; Luke
4:36). Firsthand insight growing out of experience took precedence over tradition. The apostles, like Jesus, spoke by immediate inspiration.

The apostles, like the members of the earliest
churches, were humble people (I Cor. 1:25ff.).
God was the source of their "boldness." That
"they had been with Jesus" made them unusual
persons (Acts 4:13). God made this Jesus the
"wisdom . . . righteousness . . . sanctification . . .
and redemption" for all who would exercise
faith. With insight growing out of newness of
life, the humblest Christian knew truth of which
Nicodemus, though a "ruler of the Jews," was
ignorant (John 3:1-12).

Christians like Peter and John, though "unedu-
cated, common men," were nonetheless "taught
of God." They therefore spoke what they had
"seen and heard" by divine revelation. Precisely
this made "the rulers and elders and scribes"
wonder! The world of Hellenistic culture and
Roman authority might discount the Church because of the humble status of its members. But

that world would eventually discover that, however lowly, God's "called" become instruments by whom he brings "to nothing things that are." Their boast is "of the Lord" who is the "source of life" (cf. I Cor. 1:28-30).

3

DIVINE PROVIDENCE
AND THE CHURCH

ACTS 4:32 TO 5:42

God's Best Answer to Prayer (Acts 5:31). Luke
makes the gift of the Spirit God's best answer to
prayer (Luke 11:13). Prayerful thanksgiving at
the release of Peter and John was so accompanied: "When they had prayed . . . they were
all filled with the Holy Spirit" (Acts 5:31; cf.
2:1-47). Resemblances between Acts 2:1-47 and
5:31 suggest Luke's conviction that Pentecost
needs repetition, not commemoration. The quest
of dedicated men for God's immediate guidance
makes prayer the essence of vital religion. In
such vitality is to be found the explanation of
the courageous attempt of the primitive Church
to eradicate poverty as a contradiction of spirituality.

*Community of Goods (Acts 4:32-35; cf. 2:43-
47).* Togetherness of spirit and community of
goods were felt to belong together as halves of
a whole. The Spirit's prompting explained both.
Both accounts so explain the radical sharing of

material things. Rejection from the vocabulary of Christians of the word *"own"* gave effect to Jesus' demand of any who would follow him "to deny himself and take up his cross daily" (Luke 9:23). Self-denial as self-dethronement found an impressive symbol in what the Church voluntarily did at this formative stage of its growth.

The "fear" that "came upon every soul" was "godly fear," not consternation aroused by social pressures. It was the accompaniment of Pentecost on the one hand and of the "wonders and signs" on the other which evidenced the nearness and activity of a Christlike God, who cares for men individually (Acts 2:1-4; 4:31). It was a sense of awe in the presence of the ultimate and eternal. It had the same origin as the "boldness" of Peter and John.

Under the impulse of this "godly fear," need took the place of greed as a principle of economic distribution. All hearts were "glad and generous," and a healthy spirituality purged from the "Body of Christ" all traces of infectious materialism. Neglect of human need would have left the Church indistinguishable from the world. Generosity like that disclosed in God's gift of his only-begotten Son, conformed the Church to the kingdom.

Because of this heavenly orientation of the Church, "great grace came upon all" its members, and "the Lord added to their number day by day those who were being saved" (Acts 4:33; cf. 2:47). Spiritual dynamism, not shrewd social planning, accounted for phenomenal growth. There were hidden dimensions of this growth that figures could not measure.

Identity of the Holy Spirit with the risen Christ is assumed throughout Acts. The apostles "gave their testimony to the resurrection of the Lord Jesus" because of their experience of his immediate presence as one with the Spirit. The indwelling Spirit and the indwelling Christ were indistinguishable. Lying to the Spirit and "tempting the Spirit of the Lord" were the same, and in both cases the guilty "have . . . lied . . . to God" (Acts 5:3-9). Luke is thus thoroughly trinitarian in principle.

Luke's trinitarian theism would be expected of an understudy of Paul. That apostle had identified the Spirit with the indwelling Christ. Writing to the Corinthians he had said, "Now the Lord is the Spirit . . . . And we all . . . beholding the glory of the Lord, are being changed into his likeness from one degree of glory to another; for this comes from the Lord who is the Spirit" (II Cor. 3:12-18 *passim*). Paul and Luke thus enhance and dignify the promptings of the Spirit and the leadership of Christ by making them equivalents in respect to God's own activity. Accordingly, the Church's exaltation of need over greed reflected the intention of God. It was as truly a glorification of "his servant Jesus" as the restoration to "perfect health" of the paralytic. Paralysis and greed are viewed as having a genetic relationship. Both menace spirituality and both require divine remedy. It could be appropriately said of both, "What is impossible with men is possible with God" (Luke 18:27).

Historically, community of goods was an attempt literally to perpetuate the fellowship Jesus had instituted among the Twelve. The expectation was that the framework of earthly life would shortly give place to the kingdom. Preparation for admission to that kingdom would be by living in its spirit and by its heavenly standards in advance of its actual advent.

Demonstrably, in both halves of his account of Christian beginnings, Luke arranges materials from tradition to emphasize his own passion for justice. With that much plausibility, his account of life within the Jerusalem church may be regarded as an idealized picture of how Christians ought to live together. That does not mean, however, that Luke wrote religious fiction! He was a historian as well as an evangelist. He pleaded for social redemption, but his plea had a solid historical foundation in the words and example of Jesus.

As indicated in the preface to his first volume, briefer written accounts were woven into a comprehensive story. Inclusiveness, principally, distinguishes what Luke wrote from what earlier Christians had written. Luke's use of Mark and his joint use with Matthew of a documentary account of Jesus' message illustrate his method. Instead of, like John, metamorphosing his sources, he incorporates them. The distinctive selection of materials and the very personal arrangement of them display each evangelist's own view of the gospel. But the materials themselves antedate Luke and introduce readers to primitive tradition. This means that underneath Acts 2:44-46 and 4:34ff. lie substrata of authentic history.

Little doubt exists, therefore, that the Church proposed literally to embody the new order of the coming kingdom. Community of goods was a movingly serious attempt to actualize in the corporate life of the Church the love that would be the only law in the kingdom. It expressed the Church's realistic consciousness of vocation to show the world it hoped to save the meaning of God's will in human relations.

Numerical growth and the increasingly clear prospect that history would continue required drastic modification of procedure. But this did not mean and must never mean an abandonment by the Church of responsibility to embody in its corporate life the conviction implicit in its gospel of the kingdom. Nor can the Church afford to cease urging upon the world an enthronement of spiritual values in its institutions and the dedication of material wealth to the needs of persons. By no other means can the challenge of communism be met.

Barnabas and Ananias (Acts 4:36 to 5:11). Barnabas and Ananias typify success and failure within the Church. By a play on his name, Barnabas becomes a son of *paraclesis,* a sort of "Paraclete" incarnate (cf. John 14:16,26; 15:26; 16:7). He was "a good man, full of the Holy Spirit and of faith" (Acts 11:24). His fellows could call on him for comfort, encouragement, and instruction. His faith guided by the Spirit caused him to lay "at the apostles' feet" the sale price of a piece of land.

Ananias, lacking Barnabas' faith and the Spirit bestowed on men of faith, tried to get credit for a goodness he lacked. In actuality, he opposed what the Spirit inspired the Church to attempt. His fate, like that of King Herod in Acts 12:23 became a warning to opponents of God within the Church as well as outside it (cf. Acts 5:39). His error was profounder than a merely adverse judgment on an enterprise the Church itself would soon modify. He sinned in listening to Satan instead of, like Barnabas, to the Holy Spirit

(Acts 5:3,9). The Spirit prompted complete self-surrender to Christ and a way of living that would acclimate men of faith to the kingdom. Ananias assumed the preferability of serving God *and* Mammon. In his person, as with Judas among the Twelve, the world invaded and corrupted the Church.

Ananias needed to learn, as do Christians of every generation, that what the Spirit inspires and what Jesus historically taught validate each other. The Spirit never has and never will move a man to say, "Jesus be cursed." Instead, the Spirit invariably inspires the confession, "Jesus is Lord," that is, Jesus deserves man's obedience (I Cor. 12:3). Satan, not Jesus, was Ananias' "Lord," and accordingly he undertook to "lie to the Holy Spirit."

Providence and the Apostles (Acts 5:12-42). The deaths of Ananias and Saphira illustrate God's "wrath" toward Church members who betray the self-surrender implicit in faith. Release of the apostles from prison shows God's providential care for true believers (Acts 5:19ff.).

On an occasion, when Jesus returned from the east to the west side of the Sea of Galilee, "people . . . ran about the whole neighborhood and began to bring sick people on their pallets," and they who touched even the fringe of Jesus' garment "were made well" (Mark 6:54-56). Luke does not

contain this story, but in Acts 5:12-16 tells a story
that shows a comparable effectiveness of the ministry of Peter and John. He reports that if even
so much as Peter's shadow fell upon the sick they
were made well.

Jesus' popularity, based on service to human
need, always aroused official jealousy and officious
investigation. Understandably, now, the Sad-
ducees, "filled with jealousy," had Peter and John
jailed. But neither Cross nor prison nullified
God's providence! It was not possible for Jesus
"to be held" by death because "he was not aban-
doned" by God (Acts 2:24,31). Similarly, God's
providence followed the apostles to the "common
jail," and "at night an angel of the Lord opened
the prison doors and brought them out" (Acts
5:19; cf. 12:1-19). By such stories from the
Church's past, Luke bolsters the confidence of
Christians threatened by Domitian that God ever
"keeps watch" over his own.

"The captain of the temple and the chief
priests" were as "perplexed" at the empty jail
as they had been at the empty tomb of Joseph
of Arimathea (Acts 5:24; cf. Luke 24:18-27).
"Angel of the Lord" means the manifestation of
God's power to accomplish divine purposes in
the sphere of human history. By the exertion of
that power, tomb and prison became doors to

continuing service to God, the Guardian of the Church.

The "council and all the senate of Israel" found the apostles, not in jail but "standing in the temple" teaching the people (Acts 5:25). Asked for an explanation, they replied, "We must obey God rather than men." They further justified their independence as the requirement of the Spirit God gives "those who obey him" (Acts 5:32).

Man's Wrath and God's Wisdom (Acts 5:33-39; James 1:20). The Council and Senate were "enraged" at the apostles' answer and wanted to kill them. But Gamaliel saved them from their folly. He had the wisdom to see the irresistibility of God's power. He knew history and knew that history exposed religious validity or fraud. Courageously, he based his counsel on that wisdom. For once, self-important ecclesiastics listened to sense and set the apostles free (Acts 5:40).

Fellowship in Christ's Suffering (Acts 5:40-42). Paul thought that by such sufferings as he enumerates in Second Corinthians 11:22-33 he completed "what is lacking in Christ's afflictions" (Col. 1:24). By this he did not mean to minimize the atoning significance of the Cross. Rather he insisted that the implications of the Cross must be spelled out by men of faith in life situations if the world is to be saved. Left on Calvary in the long ago, the Cross becomes impotent. Instead of being merely remembered, it must become a way of living. It must be socketed in human hearts.

Peter and John took their flogging in Paul's spirit: "They left the presence of the council, rejoicing that they were counted worthy to suffer dishonor" for Christ's sake. Instead of nursing resentment and waiting a chance to retaliate, they ceaselessly preached Jesus as Christ "in the temple and at home."

4

THE CHURCH'S
DISCOVERY OF
INCLUSIVENESS

ACTS 8:1 TO 11:26

Beginnings of Organization (Acts 6:1). The limitations imposed on men by their finiteness create problems, however good the people concerned. The very effort to implement good will involves differences of judgment. This necessitates administrative organization. Where people of differing cultural and racial traditions participate freely in community life, human frustrations are multiplied. Out of such normal gropings for sympathetic collaboration, organization emerged in the early Church.

Acts 6:1 to 11:26 sketches the expansion of the Christian movement from Jerusalem, where its members were Jews, to Antioch, where Christians were principally Greeks. Grecian Jews had early been brought into the membership of the Church. These Grecian Jews became the spiritual bridge across which the gospel reached the Gen-

tiles. The problems inherent in inclusiveness and
the account of their solution make the story of
Acts 6:1 to 11:26 epochal.

As expansion began, the Jerusalem church fell
into the background. The principal growth of the
Church was among Gentiles, with the result that
at the end of the century its membership was
largely non-Jewish. Stephen and Grecian Jews like
him spearheaded this transition. Luke sketches
the transition in seven episodes: The Hellenists
(6:1-4); spheres of service (6:5-7); acts of Stephen (6:8 to 7:60); acts of Philip (8:4-40); acts
of Saul (8:1-3; 9:1-30); acts of Peter (9:31 to
11:18); acts of the Hellenists (11:19-26). The
extensive attention to Peter, the one Palestinian
Jewish Christian in the series, shows that primitive Christianity is fulfilled, not lost, in the
transition.

The Grecian Jews (Acts 6:1-4). The majority of
Jews remained in Babylon after the Exile. They
financed the return of those who elected to live
in Palestine. They, however, continued to live
where they had rooted their lives. Later, Jews
were encouraged to settle in the principal cities
of the far-flung empire established by Alexander.
The result was that in New Testament times less
than a million of the three and a half million
Jews in the Roman Empire lived in Palestine. For
the benefit of Greek-speaking Jews outside Pales-

tine, the Holy Scriptures were translated from Hebrew into Greek. This Septuagint version of the Scriptures became the Bible of the Church during the first two centuries of Christian history.

By pilgrimage and shift of residence, Grecian Jews returned in limited numbers to Palestine. They established synagogues in Jerusalem, with services and Scriptures in Greek. Such Grecian Jews appear on the one hand to have been a fertile field for Christian evangelism and at the same time a bulwark for Judaism. Men like Stephen, Barnabas, Philip, and Saul illustrate their accessibility to the gospel. The bitterness with which other Grecian Jews attacked such Christians illustrates the zeal for Judaism that caused their return to Palestine. Paul's preconversion persecution of the Church has this explanation. The preciousness of his Jewish heritage was Paul's only adequate measure of the surpassing worth of Christianity (Phil. 3:4-11).

Yet Jews outside Palestine spoke the language of world culture and were exposed to ideas and trends of which Palestine Jews had little awareness. However much they exalted the Law, they were also exposed to non-Jewish formulations of truth. Loyalty to the Law itself led an Alexandrian Jew like Philo to interpret it in ways that never occurred to Palestinian scribes.

The implicit liberalism of Grecian Jews who

returned to Palestine had much to do with the acceptance of Christianity by some. Once converted, they saw more clearly than the Twelve the inclusiveness of the gospel. Barnabas, Stephen, Philip, and Paul illustrate this. Naturally, the Temple never occupied the place of importance for Hellenists that it held for Palestinians. The former had a natural impatience toward Temple and priesthood. This explains Stephen's alleged hostility toward Temple and ritual (Acts 6:13). His defense discloses the grain of truth in the indictment: he denies the finality of the Temple and treats it as a "way station" en route to the Church. With Paul he would hold that the true "Israel of God" is the Church (Gal. 6:16).

The synagogue was the important institution for Grecian Jews. The Scriptures and the synagogue were everywhere the foundations of Diaspora Judaism. Both had been brought back to Palestine from Babylon. Ardor for the Law was nurtured in the synagogue, so that it was no accident that animosity toward Stephen grew out of debates in synagogues of the Hellenists. The lists of those moved by inspired preaching after Pentecost and those who heard the synagogue debates make interesting parallels (Acts 2:5-11; 6:8-10): Freedmen, Cyrenians, Alexandrians, Cilicians.

Freedmen were Romans, and their synagogue was probably the place where Stephen kept his membership. He with his fellows could have been among the "visitors from Rome" mentioned in Acts 2:10. They probably decided to remain in Jerusalem, perhaps in part because of the attraction of the emerging Christian movement.

Incorporation of large numbers of these Hellenists created problems that required the appointment of the Seven as associates of the Twelve. The Hellenists thought their poor were neglected. The effort to make the community of goods permanent policy could also have created friction. These Christians from abroad whose language and Scriptures were Greek were naturally and even needlessly sensitive toward management by Aramaic-speaking "old timers." To compose such differences, a simple form of organization began.

Spheres of Service Defined (Acts 6:5-7). Differences between Grecian and Palestinian Christian Jews were probably not limited to administration. This comes out in the aftermath of the appointment of the Seven. Ostensibly responsible for the oversight of social services, they actually distinguished themselves in evangelism. The Twelve seem to have functioned as they usually had. The distinction between the Twelve and the Seven, therefore appears to have been more jurisdictional than functional.

Differing spheres of service more nearly than a shift of duties gave both groups of leaders a

reason for being. Palestinian Jewish Christianity
continued to be the sphere of primary interest for
the Twelve, while work among Grecian Jews was
undertaken by the Seven. In the vigorous prose-
cution of the latter responsibility, Stephen lost
his life.

A type of Christianity divergent at points from
its primitive form was apparently emerging
among believers of non-Palestinian origin. To the
credit of the Jerusalem leaders, full freedom was
given these Hellenistic Christians. The jurisdic-
tionalism already mentioned implemented that
freedom. This freedom was fruitfully affirmed in
the decision of the Jerusalem Council of Acts
15:25ff.

The Acts of Stephen (Acts 6:8 to 7:60). Instead
of devoting himself to business administration
Stephen became a disturbing preacher. Responsibility for care of the poor, however, probably
added realism and eloquence to his exposition of
the gospel. Opponents who brought about his
death were emissaries of the High Priest, not the
apostles. The issue was Stephen's evangelism, not
his finances. His defense of himself supplies the
only data for a reconstruction of the situation.

Suborned witnesses alleged blasphemy against
the Temple (Acts 6:11,13; cf. John 2:19). Stephen and John understood that Jesus contem-
plated displacement of the Temple with imme-

diate spiritual fellowship between God and man. The paraphernalia of religion thus became instrumental and temporary. This position Stephen espoused (Acts 7:48ff.).

Stephen states his position by means of historical retrospect comparable to that found in Hebrews. The episodes selected are Abraham's call, Moses' leadership, Solomon's building of the Temple. The point Stephen makes is that "the Most High does not dwell in houses made with hands" (Acts 7:48). This meant that Israel's leaders and institutions were preparatory and that Israel's quest was spirituality (cf. Heb. 1: 1-4; 3:5-6; 6:20; 7:28; 8:2-13). That quest culminated in Christianity. Israel's history had been a long continued but hitherto frustrated effort to actualize divine vocation. Each time the goal seemed realizable it receded. At long last came fruition in Christ. All antecedents were foreshadowings of the finality, which was Christianity: the Church was the "Israel of God" (cf. Gal. 6:16).

Stephen's logic and the viewpoint of the author of Hebrews are the same. Stephen came from Rome, and Hebrews is the earliest embodiment of the Christianity that emerged in the Roman church. That church must have originated at about the same time as the churches at Damascus and Antioch and was a generation old when

Paul wrote to them at the close of his third missionary journey. Roman Christianity, which was to set the pattern for Western Europe until the Reformation, was apparently little influenced by Paul. It continued along lines determined by its pre-Pauline leadership. Its emphases were those of the Hellenistic section of the Jerusalem church and were given wide currency when the Hellenists were scattered by the "great persecution" (Acts 8:1).

The Acts of Philip (Acts 8:4-40). Stephen, Nicolaus, and Philip among the Seven developed notable leadership. The other four remained hardly more than names. Perhaps they became entirely absorbed in administrative duties.

Nicolaus was the one non-Jew among them. He was "a proselyte of Antioch" (Acts 6:5). When the "great persecution" scattered the Hellenists, Nicolaus probably returned to Antioch and helped establish the great church whence Paul and Barnabas went on their missionary journeys. At Antioch, followers of Jesus were first called "Christians" (Acts 11:26). There also, Matthew, most popular of the Gospels, was written in about 75 A.D. Nicolaus, like Stephen and Philip, was notable for his inspired preaching and must have helped lay the foundations for the world outreach of the Mother Church of Missions.

Like Nicolaus, Philip took the gospel outside Jewry. The story of his activities in Samaria has more than a narrative interest. In understandable bitterness, a woman of Samaria said to Jesus, "Jews have no dealings with Samaritans." The Twelve, returning from Sychar reflect this bias in their amazement at finding Jesus treating a Samaritan woman as a person (John 4:9ff.). Knowing that "God is a spirit" and desires worship that is spiritual, Jesus shared the "water of life" with the woman, and a multitude of Samaritans discovered in him "the Savior of the world" (John 4:42). Samaritans had not been allowed, like Nicolaus, to become "proselytes." They were without hope of salvation.

But Philip ignored traditional bias and "proclaimed . . . Christ" in Samaria, and Samaritan multitudes "with one accord gave heed" to his message (Acts 8:5-8). Jesus had himself made it clear that faith alone counted with God and had included Samaria in his commission (Acts 1:8). Philip's campaign in Samaria, therefore, means that the gospel is on its way "to the end of the earth."

As though preaching to Samaritans were not enough, Philip next explained the Scriptures to an Ethiopian eunuch, "a minister of Candace the queen of the Ethiopians, in charge of all her treasure." Not only so, but he baptized the eunuch with the approval of "the Spirit of the Lord," and then preached the gospel at Azotus and Caesarea.

The Ethiopian appears to have been a "proselyte," and had been to Jerusalem to worship in the limited way open to "proselytes." But for a eunuch these limitations were doubly rigid (Deut. 23:1). Philip, however, knew that Christianity ignored all non-spiritual impediments. Accordingly, with the Spirit's sanction, he brushed aside legalism and racism, such as had handicapped Jewish missions, because he knew they would also obstruct the gospel's line of march "to the end of the earth."

Ethiopia designated all of Africa south of Egypt. Accordingly, the event on that desert road "that goes down from Jerusalem to Gaza" planted the gospel in the heart of a continent! Applicable here is the analogy used by Emerson in 1875 at the dedication of French's statue to "The Minute Man at Concord": "The thunderbolt falls on an inch of ground but the light of it fills the horizon."

The Acts of Peter (Acts 9:11 to 11:18). The "Acts of Paul" belong more appropriately to the discussion of "Providence and Persecution," and so are deferred to the next chapter. Peter's inspired perception that "God shows no partiality, but that in every nation anyone who fears him and does what is right is acceptable to him" unifies the events that compose Acts 9:11 to 11:18.

The climax of the section is the baptism of Cornelius and the bestowal of the Holy Spirit "on the Gentiles." The epochal outcome was that the apostles "and the brethren . . . in Judea" officialized Peter's position, saying, "To the Gentiles also God has granted repentance unto life" (Acts 10:44-48; 11:18).

The doors of the Church had been opening wider. Nicolaus, a Samaritan multitude, and an Ethiopian eunuch had been welcomed. Most impressively, however, Cornelius symbolized the world of the uncircumcised. He was "a centurion of what was known as the Italian Cohort" (Acts 10:1). Peter confronting Cornelius brings the Church face to face with the Roman world and universal humanity. Nor did the Church fail her Lord, though her agony was reminiscent of Gethsemane.

Lydda was predominantly Jewish. Thence, Peter went to Joppa on the road to Caesarea. The geography suggests allegory. At Joppa, Peter was the guest of Simon, *a tanner!* Such was the setting of the vision calling on a Jew like Peter to eat disallowed food (Acts 10:9-16). The Spirit's leadership is effective, yet follows the patient rule of "easy steps for little feet." That Peter "never had eaten anything . . . common and unclean" need not mean that he never would! The Spirit of him who "declared all foods clean" gave the orders, and leaders of the Church obeyed (Mark 7:19).

The stories of Acts 9:11 to 11:18 exhibit three emphases: (1) The compassion of Jesus permeates his Church. (2) Racism and legalism are invalid as conditions of membership in that Church. (3) A Roman centurion's acceptance of baptism refutes suspicion of the Church as seditious.

The Acts of the Hellenists (Acts 11:19-26). The death of Stephen was in a sense the re-enactment of Calvary. "His face was like that of an angel," and the quality of his spirit matched his appearance as he prayed, "Lord do not hold this sin against them" (Acts 7:54-60). The scattering of the Hellenists was Stephen's bequest to the world.

Philip went to Samaria, but the impact of his witness extended to the heart of Africa. Others like him "traveled as far as Phoenicia and Cyprus and Antioch speaking the word" (Acts 11:19). Jews and Gentiles benefitted by evangelism that respected all men as persons.

Four groupings are distinguishable in the audience of Christ's witnesses, as Luke tells the story of the Church's growth: Palestinian Jews, Grecian Jews, God-fearing Gentiles like Nicolaus who became "proselytes," and Gentiles untouched by Judaism who as pagans responded to the appeal of the gospel.

"The hand of the Lord" (i.e., God's potent support and guidance) was with those who enlarged the circle of Christian evangelism, and "a great number turned to the Lord" (Acts 11:22). Success showed God's sanction. Concretely, at Antioch "men of Cyprus and Cyrene . . . spoke to the Greeks." That God convincingly approved this approach to the Greeks means that in Acts 13:46 Paul acted on sound precedent. He was no innovator. Luke intended to show that Paul represented the basic position of the Church. His critics were "false brethren," not accredited leaders (Gal. 2:2,11). After Pentecost, and in ever enlarging circles, the Church is shown to have become inclusive.

5

PROVIDENCE AND PERSECUTION

ACTS 8:1-4; 9:1-31; 12:1-25

Origin and Objects of Persecution (Acts 8:1-4).
The first persecution of the Church was ecclesiastical. It was an extension of the Sanhedrin's
opposition to Jesus. It began in a Grecian Jewish synagogue and was directed against Greek-
speaking Jews who had accepted Christianity.
The Apostles and other Aramaic-speaking Christians conformed sufficiently in way of life and
Temple attendance to be indistinguishable from
other Jews. Judaism itself allowed for great theo-
logical variety, so that Palestinian Jewish Christians appeared to be a sect within the Jewish
church. That Saul had no previous contact with
the Twelve and "was . . . not known by sight to
the churches of Christ in Judea" indicates that
Grecian Jewish Christians bore the brunt of
persecution (Gal. 1:22).

Saul's supervision of Stephen's stoning suggests
that he was the Sanhedrin's principal lieutenant
in clearing Palestine of Hellenistic Christians

(Acts 8:1). Thereafter, he is said to have "laid waste the Church" inside and outside Palestine (Acts 8:3; Gal. 1:23; Phil. 3:6). The analogies liken him to a wild boar on a rampage and to unrestrained soldiers looting a city (cf. Psalm 80:13). Public disgrace, confiscation of property, imprisonment were penalties he invoked. Stephen alone was put to death.

Extent of the Persecution (Acts 9:1-31). Once "the churches . . . in Judea" had been purged, Saul's wrath fell upon Hellenist churches in foreign cities. Beside himself with "zeal," he obtained authorization to extend his crusade beyond Palestine (Acts 9:1; Phil. 1:6). Diaspora Jews were religiously within the jurisdiction of Palestinian Jewish authorities. They acknowledged that jurisdiction by pilgrimages and by financial subsidies to Palestinian institutions and causes. On such grounds, Saul's commission was legitimate. Regarding Samaria and Ethiopia as of secondary importance, Saul selected great urban centers as targets even as he did later when establishing Christian churches. Damascus, Alexandria, Antioch, and Rome all had large colonies of Grecian Jews, and they very early became centers of Christian missions. By his energy as a persecutor, Saul inadvertently contributed to transplanting the Church to such cities.

Damascus illustrates, but did not mark, the

limits of Christian growth in such great cities. It
is first brought under consideration because of its
proximity to Palestine. That Christianity established itself in this ancient capital of Syria at
about the same time as at Alexandria, Antioch,
and Rome is highly probable. In all such centers,
Christians might have felt the scourge of Saul's
wrath had not the course of his life been changed.

Outside Palestine, Christianity was from the
start an urban movement. Population, culture,
wealth, government were centered in the cities.
People in the hinterland remained largely untouched by world trends. In fact, the English
word "pagan" comes from the Greek word for
"rural." The countryman was a *paganus* because
he lived outside the cities and so was untouched,
unimportant, and uninfluential. Christ's "witnesses" properly concentrated their efforts in the
great cities of the Mediterranean world. Without
pressing the analogy unduly, the Church in the
increasingly urbanized world of the twentieth
century will profit by a critical reappraisal of its
strategy, agonizing though it be.

Damascus was situated just north of the Decapolis, where Jesus did much of his teaching.
It was about fifty miles from the vicinity of Tyre
and Sidon (Mark 7:24-31; Luke 10:13) and ap-
proximately thirty miles from Caesarea Philippi
where Peter's "confession" and the Transfigura-

tion took place (Luke 9:18-36). Damascenes could thus have been in the multitudes who listened to Jesus. Probably, too, Jewish pilgrims from Damascus observed the first Pentecost. That Damascus was in close touch with Jerusalem is shown by the fact that news of Saul's commission reached Ananias in advance of the crusader's own arrival (Acts 9:13f.).

Antioch, where Jesus' followers were first called Christians, lay a hundred and fifty miles northeast of Damascus. Around the close of the fourth century B.C., Antioch on the Orontes river supplanted Damascus as capital of Syria. But today Antioch is unimportant, while Damascus remains a great city. Damascus' greatness in antiquity and its continuing durability were due to natural advantages. It was located in an immense oasis created by the Abana and Pharpar rivers (cf. II Kings 5:12). A great caravan route known as the "Way to the Sea" connected the East and the Southwest. It touched the Sea of Galilee on the northwest, passed through Galilee to Esdraelon and thence connected with the coastal highway to Egypt. Damascus was included in the league of Hellenistic cities that composed the Decapolis and served them as a frontier bulwark against invaders from the East.

Between Pentecost and Saul's conversion, Damascus became an outpost also for the Church, supplying "witnesses" along a thoroughfare reaching from Egypt to the Tigris and Euphrates valley. Here geography becomes symbolic. Jerusalem, whence Saul started, was barren, rocky, scant of vegetation. Damascus, whither he journeyed, was a luxuriant oasis where he intended to create devastation. Fed by snows on Mount Hermon, two rivers lost themselves to make the desert bloom. Centuries later Mohammed, viewing the scene, said that as he expected to enter Paradise only once he would stay outside Damascus. Toward such a city, Saul, inwardly barren, moved into a sort of oasis of the spirit and thereafter was a new man in Christ.

At the time, Saul is described as a "young man" (Acts 7:58; 8:1). The Greek word *neanias* more nearly describes a man in his prime than a teen-ager (cf. Matt. 19:20ff.). Significant information from Paul's letters fills out Luke's terse description (II Cor. 11-12; Gal. 1 and 2; Phil. 3). Three epochs in his life may be distinguished: Saul the Pharisee, Saul the humble convert, Paul the slave and apostle of Jesus Christ.

The Pharisee (Acts 8:1-4; 9:1-3). The story begins with Saul the zealous Pharisee. He was a Grecian Jew, "a citizen of no mean city," Tarsus. Tarsus was an ancient city, the provincial capital of Cilicia, an educational center second only to Athens and Alexandria, according to the historian Strabo. Saul, however, emphasizes his Jewishness, not his Hellenism. "A Hebrew sprung from Hebrews," "a Pharisee, a son of Pharisees," "of the tribe of Benjamin," "touching the Law, blameless." Thus he prefers to describe himself.

To this self-description, Luke adds that he was a Roman citizen (Acts 16:37ff.; 22:25ff.). Of ways whereby citizenship might have been acquired by Saul's father, the statement to Lysias more nearly suggests distinguished service rather than purchase. As an heir to citizenship, Saul's Roman name would be *Paulos,* and by this name Luke calls him after his conversion. Paul uses his Roman name regularly in his letters. He relinquished his Jewish name with the rest of his Jewishness, once he espoused a faith wherein "neither circumcision nor uncircumcision is of any avail, but faith working through love" (Gal. 3:28; 5:6; Col. 3:11).

The Humble Convert (Acts 9:8-19; cf. I Cor. 3:5ff.; II Cor. 4:6; 5:12-15; Phil. 1:21-26; 2:3-11). Three accounts of Paul's conversion appear in Acts (9:3-9; 22:6-11; 26:12-18). These accounts agree that it took place en route to Damascus. They agree also in their use of the symbolism of "light from heaven" indicative of God's initiative. They differ regarding awareness of the light: the first account says the light flashed about Saul, his companions "hearing a voice but seeing no one"; in the second instance, the companions "saw the light but did not hear the voice"; finally, the light shone around Saul and his companions, but Saul alone heard the voice.

Paul's letters contain informative allusions to the event. Most comprehensive is his statement in Second Corinthians 4:6: "It is the God who said, 'Let light shine out of darkness,' who has shone in our hearts to give the light of the knowledge of the glory of God in the face of Christ." More than this, Paul insists, the experience acquainted him with Jesus and determined the message he preached (Gal. 1:12ff.; I Cor. 9:1; 15:8). His apostolic commission also grew out of this Damascus road event (Rom. 1:5). Using the analogy of a prize in an athletic contest, Paul says, "Christ Jesus . . . made me his own" (Phil. 3:12). Closely related to the inner meaning of this analogy is Paul's description of himself as Christ's "slave" (Rom. 1:1; Phil. 1:1). Being thus captured or enslaved, Paul on his part "presses on" to make his *own* "the prize of the call of God in Christ Jesus" (Phil. 3:14).

Paul's firsthand accounts and Luke's tradition-based reports agree on five salient points: The event took place near Damascus and changed Paul's objectives in Damascus; the Risen Christ acted for God in the situation; the experience was sudden and transforming; what happened involved two-way communication, that is, revelation and commitment; finally, it had to be shared —salvation and world service were halves of an indissoluble whole.

Saul Becomes Paul the Apostle (Acts 9:15-30). The Old Testament abounds in parallels of the sort of encounter Saul's conversion involved, such as the call of Samuel (I Sam. 3:1-10), the Son of Kish (I Sam. 10:9-13), the summons of Moses (Exod. 3:1-12), Elisha (I Kings 19:11-21), Isaiah (Isa. 6:1-8), Ezekiel (Ezek. 1:1 to 2:3); Amos (Amos 7:14-16); Jonah (Jonah 1:1-3; 3:1-5); and, most impressively similar, Jeremiah (Jer. 1:2-10).

Ananias, "a . . . disciple at Damascus," had a vision and commission that complemented Paul's and helped implement God's intention (Acts 9: 10-19). His gentle hand on the penitent's shoulder and his salutation "Brother Saul" became the human means whereby the apostle-to-be was "filled with the Holy Ghost." Thus did the crusading persecutor succumb to the "power of God unto salvation" and become Christ's "ambassador." The transformation suggests the folly of opposing God (Acts 5:40).

Herod Opposes the Apostles (Acts 12:1-25; cf. Jos. Antiq. xix. 8.2). Agrippa I was the grandson of Herod the Great. He had largely been reared at Rome and was the close friend of the youthful

Caligula. When the latter became emperor, Herod Agrippa was made governor of the territory that had been the tetrarchy of Philip. Galilee and Perea were subsequently added to his domain, and the title of "King" was conferred on him. At Caligula's death, Agrippa helped persuade the Senate to select Claudius as emperor, and in gratitude Claudius added Samaria and Judea to Herod's kingdom. This explains how the apostles at Jerusalem came under his jurisdiction.

That James and Peter had belonged to the inner circle of the Twelve made them logical targets for a super-patriotic politician. He intended to use them to enhance his position with the Temple hierarchy and at Rome. Having killed James, Herod "proceeded to arrest Peter." Then the unpredictable happened: God interposed his power, and Herod found himself helpless. Not only so, but "the chains fell off Peter's hands." Prison doors swung open, and "the Angel of the Lord" left Herod only an empty jail. That deliverance was God's work, and the Church knew it (Acts 12:11ff.). Blind to the meaning of the event, Herod executed the helpless jailers, and hastened his own doom.

In the vicinity of Tyre and Sidon, within a few miles from Caesarea Philippi, the scene of Peter's "Great Confession," Herod permitted the acclamation of his oration as "The Voice of God." His folly called down upon him the "wrath of God," with the result that "an angel of the Lord smote him . . . and he was eaten by worms and died." His fate illustrated the reverse side of God's providence. Thus was "the wrath of man" made to praise God (cf. Psalm 76:10). For the Church in Luke's time, threatened by the fury of the insane Domitian, such accounts of God's providence in earlier days encouraged and sustained the faith of believers.

GOD REQUIRES AN INCLUSIVE CHURCH

The Spirit Authorizes the Gentile Mission (Acts 13:1-3). The greatest crisis Christianity faced in the first century emerged in the controversy over admission of Gentiles to the Church. The issue was whether the Church, like the synagogue, would wear the garb of racism or whether spiritual fitness alone counted. The decision was that all included in God's redeeming love must be eligible for membership in *his* Church on the sole condition of *faith.* That decision was reached gradually and through great travail of spirit. It awaits complete implementation today.

The requirement had been that Gentiles desiring membership in the synagogue must symbolically join the Jewish race. That was the meaning of the requirement that proselytes be circumcised. A considerable number of Gentiles acquiesced in this demand. But a larger number declined, and Jewish missions suffered an insurmountable handicap because of this racial barrier.

That Judaism was ardently missionary is implied in Jesus' severe criticism: "You traverse sea and land to make a single proselyte, and when he has become a proselyte, you make him twice as much a child of hell as yourselves" (Matt. 23:15). That Saul was a Jewish missionary when converted individualizes that fervor to evangelize the world.

Gentiles willing to accept the ethical monotheism of Judaism but unwilling to become racially Jewish were called "God Fearers" in distinction from "proselytes." That they composed a considerable proportion of synagogue congregations is highly probable. Paul customarily singled them out when speaking in synagogues, and among them he seems to have won his first converts in cities where he founded churches. The prominence of Paul's appeal to "God Fearers" characterizes Luke's account of his synagogue preaching (Acts 13:16, etc.).

With his own experience as a Jewish missionary to guide him and with his clear perception of the spirituality of God's requirements, Paul took the lead in striking the shackles of racism from Christian missions. He was by no means the only missionary to the Gentiles. He became known as "The Apostle to the Gentiles" par excellence because of his successful fight to make faith alone the condition of salvation and of full membership in all churches. Above all others, he made the Church see that "he is a true Jew who is one inwardly, and real circumcision is a matter of the heart, spiritual and not literal" (Rom. 2:29). What made Paul unashamed to preach the gospel at Rome, the world's "melting pot," was that in it at long last was disclosed a way of approval before God that was based exclusively on faith and so equally open to human beings as such (Rom. 1:16f.).

It is no accident that at Antioch, where the issue was raised and where it was settled on Paul's terms, "the disciples were first called Christians." Settlement in terms of "the mind of Christ" merited that designation (Acts 11:26; cf. I Cor. 2:16; Phil. 2:5). Perhaps it remains the timeless condition of being so designated—Christians.

Luke indicates how gradually the issue emerged. Grecian Jews had participated in Pentecost. One of the Seven was a Greek by race, Nicolaus. Then Peter had discovered the iniquity of calling any man common and "unclean" in view of God's readiness to bestow the Holy Spirit "even on Gentiles" (Acts 10:28,45; 11:9). Finally came the great break-through at Antioch when "a great number . . . turned to the Lord" when men from Cyprus and Cyrene "spoke to the Greeks" (Acts 11:20f.).

That news caused the Jerusalem church to dispatch Barnabas to Antioch. This mission was the occasion on which Barnabas went to Tarsus "to look for Saul" (Acts 11:22ff.). The entire sequence of events is Luke's preface to the missionary journeys of Acts 13:1 to 20:38.

The Holy Spirit, not the church at Antioch, authorized those journeys. The church "set . . . Barnabas and Saul apart," but their task was God's assignment. Their accomplishments, too, were what "God had done with them" (Acts 13:1-3; 14:27). God set their task, and God "opened a door of faith to the Gentiles."

A Triumphant Beginning on Cyprus (Acts 13:4-12). Seleucia was the seaport for Syrian Antioch. It was sixteen miles west of Antioch and five miles north of the mouth of the Orontes, where silt from the river did not impede larger ships. There Barnabas, Mark, and Paul embarked for Cyprus. Cyprus was an important source of timber and the principal source of copper for the Mediterranean world. Great copper deposits determined the island's name. Originally, it had been an imperial province, incorporated with Cilicia, Saul's home province. In 22 B.C., it was made a senatorial province and so was administered by a proconsul.

Barnabas, the outstanding Hellenist in the membership of the Jerusalem church, was a native of Cyprus (Acts 4:36). Men of Cyprus and Cyrene "spoke to the Greeks" at Antioch (Acts 11:20). Nowhere could Barnabas, Mark, and Paul more appropriately have begun their initial missionary journey. This first lap of their journey took the missionaries a hundred and fifty miles southwest to Salamis, the easternmost port of Cyprus.

What they did as well as what they said is described as "the teaching of the Lord" (Acts 13:12). The two items of principal importance in the Cyprus campaign are that henceforth Saul becomes Paul, and Sergius Paulus the Roman proconsul "sought to hear the word of God" (Acts 13:1,7,13).

In the person of Sergius Paulus, Christianity dramatically confronted Roman authority and aristocracy. Correspondingly, and in the same setting, it confronted and defeated charlatanism in the person of Bar Jesus, whose Greek name was Elymas. That Sergius Paulus was "a man of intelligence" was calculated to command the gospel to his kind and class throughout the Empire. The spread of the Church similarly signalized the discomfiture of magic and deceit. Of no small significance, also, was the enlargement of the horizon and confidence of the apostles themselves. Their success on Cyprus contributed to their success in Galatia. The ensuing account of new triumphs is effectively prefaced by this story of the conversion of a Roman proconsul. Both governor and apostle, by interesting coincidence, were Roman citizens and bore the name of *Paulos*.

The Campaign in Galatia (Acts 13:13 to 14:28). Migrating hordes of Gauls from western Europe in 390 B.C. almost took the city of Rome. Driven off, they moved eastward and, between 281 and 239 B.C., overran Asia Minor. Defeated by Attalus of Pergamum in 239, they were forced to settle in a district north and east of the center of the peninsula. To the north lay Bithynia. Cappadocia and Lycaonia were neighbors on the south. Phrygia lay to the west. To this area was given the name "Galatia." That designation was later applied to a much more extensive area under Roman rule after 189 B.C. After 25 B.C., the Roman province of Galatia stretched from Bithynia entirely through the peninsula to Pamphylia. In the southwest part of this Roman province were the cities visited by Paul and Barnabas according to Acts 13:13 to 14:28. To the churches established there, Paul addressed the earliest of his letters, Galatians (Gal. 1:2).

Twice on this journey the missionaries visited the Galatian churches (Acts 14:21). Sufficient time elapsed between those visits to make them distinct and to suggest identification with the two visits implied in Gal. 4:13, where the "former"

of two visits is meant. This means that Galatians
was written on Paul's return to Syrian Antioch in
Acts 14:28 and just before he started to Jerusalem
for the visit described in Acts 15. Of Paul's two
visits to Jerusalem since his conversion, that of
Galatians 1:18 is to be equated with Acts 9:26ff.
and that of Galatians 2:1 with Acts 11:30 and
12:25.

At Perga, John Mark left the expedition (Acts
13:13). The cause of his defection has usually
been regarded as homesickness. Much more
probably Mark's provincial outlook made Paul's
rejection of racism distasteful to him. He shared
the limitations of Peter and the real, but less
rigid, reservations of Barnabas (Acts 10:9-16;
Gal. 2:11-16). He may also have felt that their
commission from the church at Antioch limited
them to Cyprus. This, reinforced by his personal
racial bias, caused him to hesitate to turn so
definitely to the Gentiles as the expedition to
Galatia involved. What he overlooked was that
the Holy Spirit was giving the orders and that
the Church was Christ's, not the possession of
those who composed its membership. Paul's
severity suggests this sort of apostasy on the
younger man's part (Acts 15:37ff.). A chastened
and matured Mark later proved his fitness to become the apostle's trusted fellow worker (Col.
4:10; Philemon 24; II Tim. 4:11).

Paul and Barnabas appear merely to have passed through Perga, although it was the capital of Pamphylia. Their haste probably grew out of eagerness to reach Ephesus, which except for Rome and Alexandria was the greatest city of the Mediterranean world.

The great Roman road from Syrian Antioch to Ephesus ran through the Cilician Gates and Pisidian Antioch. Ephesus was to be the climax of Paul's whole career. He did not reach it until his third missionary journey, but it beckoned him from the start. With Ephesus as his real goal, he stopped at Pisidian Antioch and there, as later at Troas, the Spirit diverted him to a divinely determined itinerary (Acts 16:6-10).

Antioch was located in the corner of Phrygia touching Pisidia and is called "Pisidian Antioch" to distinguish it from Syrian Antioch, whence the missionaries started. This part of Phrygia had been integrated with the Roman province of Galatia and is most accurately designated Galatian Phrygia (Acts 16:16). Augustus made it a Roman colony and settled many army veterans there. This gave it a definitely Roman character.

Antiochus IV (175-163 B.C.) had annexed Palestine to Syria and tried to destroy Judaism as a religion. He desecrated the Temple, forbade circumcision and observance of the Sabbath, and made it a crime to possess any portion of the

written Law. His repressive measures brought
about the Maccabaean revolt, whose outcome
was the achievement of religious and political
freedom for the Jews, the latter to be ended only
by the coming of the Romans under Pompey in
63 B.C. Part of Antiochus' campaign of intimida-
tion had been the forced emigration of two
thousand Jewish families to Pisidian Antioch.
Descendants of these families composed the Jewish community when Paul and Barnabas visited
the city. Their background explains the violence
with which Antiochian Jews reacted against the
gospel: they had suffered too much for their
Jewish faith to give it up easily.

On the Sabbath, Paul spoke by invitation in
the Antiochian synagogue. His sermon as reported by Luke follows the same essential pattern as the sermons of Peter and Stephen. That
resemblance, coupled with dissimilarity to Paul-
ine Christianity as seen first hand in the apostle's
letters, justifies the conclusions regarding all the
speeches in Acts as stated in the Introduction
to this *Guide*.

Inclusion of "God Fearers" in the address of
the sermon emphasizes the presence of non-Jewish worshipers in most Diaspora synagogues.
Their enthusiastic reception of the message of
the visitors contributed to the emotional animosity of the Jewish majority in the congregation

(Acts 13:16, 43-50). The result was the apostolic declaration, "We turn to the Gentiles."

That declaration is the most significant item in the record of the stay at Antioch. It was surely not the beginning of the Gentile mission. Yet it is definitely a milestone in the growth of the Church. Apparently Luke understood it to be the inauguration of a policy of establishing churches clearly and corporately distinguishable from synagogues. Christianity was no longer to be considered a movement within Judaism, but a religious community possessing its own autonomy. This is the clear advance Luke associates with the founding of the Galatian churches. He underscores that judgment with an interesting quotation from Isaiah 49:6, interpreted in effect to mean that the Church henceforth is "the Israel of God" (cf. Gal. 6:16).

From Pisidian Antioch, Paul and Barnabas traveled eighty-five miles southeast to Iconium (Acts 14:1ff.). Iconium was the head of a tetrarchy of fourteen Lycaonian towns, all of which had been made a part of Galatia under the rule of Amyntas. When the emperor Claudius later divided Galatia, Iconium became the capital of Lycaonia and the residence of the proconsul. In the local synagogue on the Sabbath, the "God Fearers" heard the missionaries with customary cordiality. The threat of molestation by "unbelieving Jews," however, caused the apostles to flee to "Lystra and Derbe . . . and there they preached the gospel" (Acts 14:6f.).

Lystra was twenty miles from Iconium, and Derbe was thirty miles beyond in the same southerly direction. Lystra had been made a Roman colony by Augustus, and this gave it a definitely Roman character. Paul's restoration of a lame Lystran closely parallels Peter's similar cure at the entrance to the Temple (Acts 3:2-8). This is more than a coincidence: Luke intends thereby to show that "since God is one . . . he shows no partiality" and is equally the God of Gentiles and Jews (cf. Romans 2:11; 3:29-31). Adoration of the visitors as though they were Zeus and Hermes bore eloquent testimony to their popularity. The Lystran audience was entirely pagan, which made their cordiality especially noteworthy (Acts 14:15-17; cf. 13:46).

Bitter enemies from Iconium, however, invaded Lystra and created violence that almost equaled the tragedy of Stephen's stoning. The conversion of Timothy was a notable monument to success at Lystra (Acts 16:3). As Stephen's stoning had indelibly affected Saul, so Paul's stoning stirred the youthful Timothy.

Timothy was a person of mixed race. Since, however, Christianity disregarded race, this caused him no embarrassment. Eunice, one of the

few Jews at Lystra, had married a Greek, and
in this way she may have followed the example
of Lois. The significant thing about them was
their "faith," and of that "heavenly treasure"
they left Timothy a notable legacy (II Tim. 1:5).
That inheritance contributed to Timothy's becoming Paul's "true child in the faith" and his
trusted assistant (Rom. 16:21; I Cor. 16:10; II
Cor. 1:1, etc.). No details of the stay at Derbe
are given, but the over-all summary for Lystra
and Derbe is that Paul and Barnabas "made
many disciples" (Acts 14:21).

From Derbe, the apostles might understandably have taken the Roman road southeastward
to Tarsus and thence to Syrian Antioch, whither
they went eventually (Acts 14:24-28). But "anx-
iety for all the churches" made it Paul's practice
to revisit and "strengthen" churches he had
founded (Acts 15:41). Therefore they retraced
their steps to Lystra, Iconium, Pisidian Antioch,
and Perga. They then took ship for Seleucia and
went thence to Antioch in Syria. For the further
conservation of the results of evangelism, the
apostles "appointed elders . . . in every church
. . . and committed them to the Lord," the true
Head of the Church to which they all belonged
(Acts 14:23).

7

CHRISTIANS IN
CONFERENCE

ACTS 15:1-35

Report to the Church (Acts 14:27-28). The
church at Syrian Antioch, in obedience to the
Spirit, had "set apart" Barnabas and Saul for a
divinely assigned task (Acts 13:2). By its action,
the church released them from the local duties of
"prophets and teachers" which had been their
responsibility along with "Symeon who was called
Niger, Lucius of Cyrene, and Manaen a member
of the court of Herod the tetrarch" (Acts 13:1).
The import of this "setting apart" was simply
that the local church relieved the two selectees
from ecclesiastical duties at Antioch (cf. Rom.
1:1). That negative function belonged to the
Church. But the task to which Barnabas and
Saul were thus surrendered was determined by
God: the Spirit "called" them and bestowed the
wisdom they needed.

Their task is now completed. For courtesy's
sake and to upbuild the faith of the Church, they
appropriately "gathered the Church together"

and declared "all that God had done with them" (Acts 14:27).

This apostolic report involved two emphases. It reflected the humility exemplified by the Lord of the Church and expected of his apostles (Mark 8:35; 10:35ff.; John 13:3-17; Phil. 2:3-11). Barnabas and Paul take no credit for the churches founded and the multitudes evangelized. All this was "what God had done with them." But Luke also has in mind an impact on the non-Christian public. Increasingly, Roman officialdom was becoming suspicious of the Church. Tacitus, the Roman historian who wrote about 116 A.D., justified Nero's persecution on the ground that it was not "so much on the count of arson as for hatred of the human race" by Christians (*Annals* xv. 44). Pliny, Roman governor of Bithynia-Pontus in 111 A.D., wrote the emperor Trajan that he could discover in Christianity "nothing more than depraved and excessive superstition" (*Letters* X. xcvi).

On the basis of such misimpressions, Domitian, within the decade when Acts was written, launched an empire-wide attack on the Church to destroy it. To highly placed critics, Luke illustrates that emissaries of the Church are servants of God and that their activities are what "God has done with them." Implicitly he warns that opponents, whether Jews or Romans, put themselves in the unenviable position of "opposing God" (Acts 5:39).

Surely such Romans as Cornelius, Sergius Paulus, the Magistrates at Philippi, and Gallio of Corinth, to say nothing of Claudius Lysias, Felix, and Festus were sufficient to refute such calumnies. For that purpose, Luke gives them prominence in his story of Christian beginnings.

Believers Who Belonged to the Party of the Pharisees (Acts 15:1-6). After making their report, Paul and Barnabas "remained no little time" at Syrian Antioch (Acts 14:28). This means they made an unhurried visit. Numerous episodes belong to this period of rest and fellowship.

For one thing, Cephas came to Antioch (Gal. 2:11). Under the spell of his vision at Joppa (Acts 10:9), he "ate with the Gentiles" who were members of the Church. But the arrival of "believers who belonged to the party of the Pharisees" frightened him so badly that "he drew back and separated himself." Peter's shoddy example even upset Barnabas (Gal. 2:11-13). Peter and Barnabas probably excused their conduct under the necessity of "protecting their influence." Paul saw that by their human bias they grieved the Spirit. So, moved by that Spirit, he publicly rebuked Peter for being more Jewish than Christian (Gal. 2:14ff.).

But this was not all. Christians of the sort who

frightened Peter and Barnabas went to Galatia during the time required for Paul and Barnabas to return from Perga to Seleucia. They assured the newly converted Galatians that they represented the Jerusalem apostles. Also, on the authority of the Holy Scriptures, they urged the necessity of joining the Jewish race as a condition of membership in the Christian Church: no circumcision, no salvation. Paul, they recalled, had not been one of the Twelve and so knew the gospel only by hearsay.

Paul greatly desired to return to Galatia and refute his critics, as he had recently done Cephas. But this was not practicable. So he did the next best thing: he wrote them a forceful letter, our Galatians, to be read publicly in all churches. In his letter, Paul refers to his conversion as also a summons to apostleship and to his message as divinely inspired. That done, he expounds the gospel as a way of approval before God based on "faith," that is, self-surrender to Christ's Lordship (Gal. 3 to 6). Having dispatched that letter, Paul and Barnabas hurried to Jerusalem.

Conference at Jerusalem (Acts 15:6-35). Here was an issue more serious than the proverbial "tempest in a teapot." Decided wrongly, it might deprive the Church of its most distinctively Christian asset—inclusiveness. Because of its cruciality, it deserved and received serious consideration by "the apostles and elders" (Acts 15:6).

Since the embarrassing encounter at Antioch, Peter had recovered his spiritual balance. The Holy Spirit, bestowed at Pentecost and renewed at Joppa, inspired him at Jerusalem to urge constructive compromise. On the evidence that the Gentiles heard and believed the gospel and that God "gave them the Holy Spirit," Peter reasoned it would needlessly "make trial of God" to burden Gentile believers with "a yoke . . . which neither our fathers nor we have been able to bear." So to burden them would in fact contradict the Christian premise "that we . . . and they . . . will be saved through the grace of the Lord Jesus" (Acts 15:7-11).

Paul himself could not have said it better. Coming from Peter, a favorable decision by the Assembly might immediately have been expected. But this was conference, and "deliberate speed" was preferable to haste. Consequently, "all the assembly kept silence." The evidence was not all before them. The seriousness of the issue required a patient examination of that evidence. The Church clearly believed that the Holy Spirit reverenced fact rather than whimsy and that inspiration came by judicial thoughtfulness, not hysteria.

Accordingly, Barnabas and Paul were now attentively heard. Barnabas had long enjoyed respect at Jerusalem. Long known as "a good man, full of the Holy Spirit," his opinions were deservedly influential. He spoke first, and afterward Paul (Acts 15:12).

The substance of the report of both missionaries was "the signs and wonders God had done through them among the Gentiles" (Acts 15:12). Such items as the conversion of Sergius Paulus, the discomfiture of Elymas, the glorification of "the word of God" at Pisidian Antioch, the conversion of Timothy illustrated those "signs and wonders."

James, the brother of Jesus, was now head of the Jerusalem church (Gal. 1:19; 2:9). Christians who created confusion in Galatia claimed to act on his authority (Gal. 2:12). Because these "false brethren" had misrepresented him, James now spoke impressively for himself and for the Assembly. He first finds in the Scriptures inspired support for the experience reported by Peter, Barnabas, and Paul (Acts 15:16-18; cf. Jer. 12:15 and Amos 9:11, and Isa. 45:21). Inspiration both past and present thus undergirded James' conclusions.

With Scripture and apostolic testimony as a twofold foundation, James, speaking for the Assembly, said: "We should not trouble those Gentiles who turn to God" with scribal legalism (Acts

15:21). Paul could have asked for no better support. Nor could the conference method for settling controversy in the Church have had better illustration. Continuing debate might have stalled Christian expansion and left an aftermath of bitterness. Conference and reasoned decision left all parties personally free, but definitely espoused inclusiveness as the position of the Church.

That there might be no doubt what the Assembly judged to be "the wave of the future," the apostles and elders put their decision into writing and selected Judas Barsabbas and Silas to go with Paul and Barnabas to Antioch, review the proceedings at Jerusalem, and publicly read the epistle of Acts 15:22-35:

Since we have heard that some persons from us have troubled you . . . although we gave them no instructions, it seemed good to us in assembly to choose men and send them to you. . . . We have therefore sent Judas and Silas, who will . . . tell you the same things by word of mouth.

For it has seemed good to the Holy Spirit and to us to lay upon you no greater burden than these necessary things: that you abstain from what has been sacrificed to idols . . . and from unchastity.

Precedence given the Holy Spirit by James is neither incidental nor accidental, but deliberate. Remembering the solution by that conference of a touchy problem among equally good men,

Paul later urged Christians at Corinth to work out their own acute differences by similar methods. Instead of lawsuits before pagan judges, he insists that churchmen select saintly men from their own midst to adjudicate differences as befitting those who have been "washed . . . justified . . . sanctified in the name of the Lord Jesus Christ and in the Spirit of our God" (I Cor. 6:1-11). Sanctification did not prevent differences of opinion among finite men, equally good, but it did determine the brotherliness of spirit in which those differences were adjusted. The gospel is discredited when "sanctification" sets the saints quarreling and the sinners arguing.

The note about abstention "from what has been sacrificed to idols" requires special attention. Paul discussed this matter at great length in First Corinthians 8:1 to 10:33. That he devoted three chapters to the problem illustrates its seriousness. Temples in antiquity were more than places of worship: they were depositories for money, and they served as meat markets. Relatively small portions of sacrificial animals were consumed in the liturgy. Unused parts were eaten by temple personnel or put on sale. Income from such sales helped finance religious institutions. The logic of sacrifice was that in the rite of consecration, the flesh of the animal was transmuted into the substance of the Deity, so that persons eating this meat themselves became devotees more or less automatically. Out of such pagan roots, emerged sacramentalism in those branches of the Church where the eucharistic elements are supernatural-ized by consecration and therefore, when eaten, regenerate the devotee.

Paul, of course, took no stock in such naïvete. "An idol has no real existence," he says. So there can be no injury in eating meat in one's home, though bought at the temple market. "We are no worse off if we do not eat, and no better off if we do. . . . Food does not commend us to God"— only faith does that. But faith "works through love" (Gal. 5:6). Therefore, because simple Christians of pagan background may be con-fused at seeing Christian leaders eating meat from a temple market, Paul says, "We endure anything rather than put an obstacle in the way of the gospel of Christ." Or, to put it differently, "If food is a cause of my brother's falling, I will never eat meat, lest I cause my brother to fall." Summarizing the matter in First Corinthians 10, Paul conditions freedom on considerateness:

All things are lawful, but not all things are helpful . . . not all things build up. . . . Eat whatever is sold in the meat market without raising any question. . . . But if someone says to you, 'This has been offered in sacrifice,' then out of consideration for the man who informed you, and for conscience sake—I mean his conscience, not yours—do not eat it.

This means that Christians in all their activities will "do all to the glory of God."

8

ESTABLISHING THE CHURCH IN MACEDONIA AND ACHAIA

ACTS 15:36 TO 18:22

A Vital Sequel to the Jerusalem Conference (Acts 15:36-41). The conference at Jerusalem did more than iron out differences. It formulated policies that eventuated in far-flung extensions of Christian growth. Release from the racism that had hobbled Jewish missions had as its natural sequel the planting of the gospel in Macedonia and Achaia. Such a sequel bears eloquent testimony to the fruitfulness of group thinking and planning. In no other way does the Holy Spirit work more creatively.

"Strengthening" Churches by Revisitation (Acts 15:41). Paul and Barnabas now took separate paths. They had disagreed about John Mark. But they were agreed that newly founded churches needed supervision and that revisitation must complement evangelization.

Luke has told of the establishment of churches on Cyprus and in southwest Galatia (Acts 13 to 14). Indirectly, in Acts 15:41, he refers to the earlier founding of churches in Syria and Cilicia. All these churches are now included in a comprehensive campaign of revisitation. At Derbe in Galatia, Paul and Barnabas "returned to Lystra and to Iconium and to Antioch strengthening the souls of the disciples" (Acts 14:22). Now they apply that strategy on a grand scale.

For that purpose, "Barnabas took Mark . . . and sailed away to Cyprus," while "Paul chose Silas and departed" for Syria, Cilicia, and Galatia. Silas, as bearer of the Assembly's letter on racism, was a fortunate choice as Paul's helper.

The churches of Syria and Cilicia probably owed their origin to Paul's activity during the eleven-year period between the visits to Jerusalem of Galatians 1:18 and 2:1. The three years mentioned in Galatians 1:18 refer to no period of lengthy meditation in Arabia. Paul was not given to lengthy meditation: he was an activist. His own statement is that following his conversion he "went away into Arabia, and . . . returned to Damascus." The three years measures the time between conversion and the first trip thereafter to Jerusalem. Similarly, the fourteen years of Galatians 2:1 designates the interval between conversion and visit number two. Luke knows nothing of a trip to Arabia for any purpose (cf. Acts 9:20-30). A plot to kill Paul forced him to flee, but he appears from Acts to have gone to Jerusalem and thence to have returned to Tarsus.

Accordingly, then, the years between Acts 9 and 13 were spent in Syria and Cilicia doing the kind of things described in Acts 13:1 to 21:6. Thus in revisiting the churches of Syria and Cilicia, Paul worked with local Christian groups such as he had organized in Galatia. The two events of notable importance in these scenes of former labors were the selection of Timothy as a second assistant and the Spirit's insistence that the missionaries go into Macedonia instead of Asia (Acts 16:1, 6).

Compromise That Was Not Compromising (Acts 16:3). In an earlier test case, Paul refused to allow the circumcision of Titus (Gal. 2:5). They were "false brethren" who insisted on it. Acquiescence in their demands would be an unthinkable compromise of the "truth of the gospel." Now, at Lystra, with no issue raised, Paul himself has Timothy circumcised! Consent in the first instance would have involved admission of the importance of an unimportant matter. Now action in a neutral situation forestalls the exaltation of the same unimportant matter to a place of primary importance.

Pisidian Antioch was more Phrygian than Galatian. It is best described as located in Galatic Phrygia. On the first journey, Paul and Barnabas had gone directly from Perga to Antioch, probably intending to go thence to Ephesus. Instead, the Spirit diverted them southward to the cities listed in Acts 13 and 14. Now at Pisidian Antioch again, Paul is "forbidden by the Holy Spirit to speak the word in Asia" (Acts 16:6f.).

The Macedonian Vision (Acts 16:8-10). When the Spirit forbids, it is because of what he proposes. Forbidden to go to Ephesus, Paul and his party "went down to Troas." There, by symbolic vision, the Spirit disclosed the divine preference for the immediate evangelization of southeastern Europe. In the vision, a Macedonian besought Paul, "Come over to Macedonia and help us." Paul and his party thereupon "sought to go into Macedonia."

Following the decision at Troas, Luke's narrative shifts from the third person to the first person plural: "Setting sail . . . *we* made a direct voyage to Samothrace . . . and from there to Philippi" (Acts 16:11f.). Save for the last of them, these "We" sections in Acts center about Philippi. If these sections are a travel diary, and if Luke wrote Luke-Acts, it may be inferred that he became a Christian at Troas and urged Paul to bring the gospel to his home city, Philippi. The Spirit used Luke's plea in symbolic vision to induce Paul to move into Macedonia instead of Asia.

In Macedonia, Paul established churches at Philippi and Thessalonica. Letters to those churches are preserved in the New Testament. He appears to have organized a church at Beroea, but no letter remains to corroborate the implication of Acts 17:10-13.

The church at Philippi had as its nucleus a group of women who gathered each Sabbath for prayer. Lydia's home afforded the missionaries comfortable lodging. From the outset and repeatedly afterward, these good women assisted Paul financially. He refers to this as their "partnership" in the gospel and as "a fragrant offering, a sacrifice acceptable to God" (Phil. 1:5-7; 4:18). The prominence and complete freedom of women in Paul's first European church shows that the limitations advised for women at Corinth were never intended as church-wide regulations. They were required by purely local conditions and have for too long caused a tragic waste of woman power even in churches of the twentieth century.

An uproar caused by Paul's exorcism of a "spirit of divination" from an exploited slave girl caused the jailing of the missionaries. But, as with Peter in Acts 12:3-11, God's omnipresent providence opened the prison's doors, and "everyone's fetters were unfastened" (Acts 16:26). The impact of this "sign" brought about the conver-

sion of the jailer and the apologetic release of
Paul and Silas. The report of this official exoneration and of the providence that caused it were
part of Luke's message to Christians and to Roman magistrates.

Paul and Silas went to Thessalonica from
Philippi by way of Amphipolis and Apollonia. As
guests of Jason, they used the freedom of the
local synagogue to do their initial preaching.
Some Jews "were persuaded . . . as were a great
many of the devout Greeks and not a few of the
leading women . . . and joined Paul and Silas"
(Acts 17:4). But success aroused jealousy and
incited attack on Jason's house. Jason made bond
for his guests, however, and the authorities "let
them go."

The Thessalonian pattern of success and opposition was repeated at Beroea. Beroean Jews "received the word with all eagerness," and "not a
few Greek women of high standing as well as
men" became believers. But Jews from Thessalonica incited the crowds, and Paul withdrew
(Acts 17:10-15).

Achaia Evangelized (Acts 17:16 to 18:17). After
Cyprus on the first journey, the Spirit, to Mark's
displeasure, sent the missionaries to Galatia.
Now, the Spirit leads Paul and party from Macedonia into Achaia.

According to Acts, Paul went alone to Athens,

leaving Silas and Timothy to join him later. Paul himself says Timothy accompanied him to Athens and was sent thence back to Thessalonica to "exhort" and "establish" the Thessalonians (I Thess. 3:1). The difference is not great, but in such instances of divergence, Paul's own clear report is final.

Of the stay at Athens, Paul tells only of the dispatch of Timothy to Thessalonica. Luke gives the details in Acts 17:16-34. Paul first sought a hearing "with the Jews and the devout persons" in the local synagogue. He also spoke "in the market place . . . with those who chanced to be there," among them Epicurean and Stoic philosophers. These were confused by Paul's correlation of "Jesus and the Resurrection" (Acts 17:18). They apparently assumed that Anastasia was a female counterpart for Jesus, *anastasia* being the Greek word for resurrection.

That they might hear him under more favorable circumstances than the market place, these philosophers brought Paul to the Areopagus. This could mean the hill by that name located behind the market place and northwest of the Acropolis. More probably it designated the "Council of the Areopagus," which had oversight of religious and educational matters and possessed authority to examine the credentials of itinerant lecturers. Before that Council, Paul gave his address (Acts 17:22-31).

Luke's reason for emphasizing that address was to show Paul's competence to speak the language of philosophers and thus to illustrate the intellectual respectability of the gospel. Paul himself told the Corinthians, "Not many of you were wise according to worldly standards, not many were powerful, not many were of noble birth" (I Cor. 1:26ff.). The lowly undoubtedly did compose the membership of most early churches. But Luke in a later time clearly proposes to claim cultural respectability for the Church. Accordingly, he reiterates accounts of the conversion of Greeks of "high standing" (cf. Acts 13:7; 16:14; 17:12). By Paul's address, he shows the appeal of the gospel to men of "intelligence" such as composed the Council, some of whom "joined him and believed" (Acts 17:34).

The Long and Fruitful Stay at Corinth (Acts 18:1-17). From Athens, Paul went to Corinth and there labored eighteen months (Acts 18:1,11). Aquila and Priscilla, recently arrived from Rome, opened their home to him and made him a partner in their business (Acts 18:2f.). These newfound friends seem already to have been Christians. Disturbances in Italian synagogues similar to those caused by Paul's preaching at Thessalonica and Corinth probably moved Claudius to expel all Jews from Rome. To outsiders, Christians seemed to be a troublesome movement within Judaism.

Paul was well into his work at Corinth when "Silas and Timothy arrived from Macedonia" (Acts 18:5). Timothy's report on conditions and problems at Thessalonica caused Paul to write our First Thessalonians. In the main, the Thessalonian church was in good condition. Paul speaks appreciatively of their "work of faith and labor of love and steadfastness of hope" (I Thess. 1:3). Three problem groups, however, had taxed the patience of local leaders. To those leaders, Paul wrote to counteract impatience. The substance of his counsel is found in 5:14: "Admonish the idle, help the weak, encourage the fainthearted, be patient with them all." Patience for the Christian is something more than tolerant forbearance: it is essentially action that looks toward reclamation. To admonish the idle, help the weak, encourage the desponding is severally and collectively to "be patient."

Second Thessalonians was a follow-up letter to emphasize the counsel previously given regarding "the idle" and the "faint-hearted." As a supplement to "sweet reason," the apostle jolts idling, cloud-watching adventists with the partly humorous proposal, "If any one will not work, let him not eat"—a rather activistic way of showing "patience" (II Thess. 3:10). This letter got results.

At Corinth, opposition from conservative Jews stopped Paul's synagogue preaching. As in Acts 13:46, the announcement, "I will go to the Gentiles" meant the reaffirmation of a decision to establish the Church in independence of the synagogue. Yet this synagogue ministry had been fruitful: Titius Justus, a "God Fearer," and Crispus, the ruler of the synagogue, "with all his household" together with numerous other Corinthians "believed and were baptized" (Acts 18:7f.).

Such successes were not the only source of encouragement. In a vision one night, God assured the apostle, "Do not be afraid, but speak out . . . for I am with you and no man shall . . . harm you; for I have many people in this city" (Acts 18:10).

Events Test God's Promise (Acts 18:12-17). Hardly had the encouraging vision faded when events tested faith. Gallio became "proconsul of Achaia" in June 51 A.D. Paul was then nearing the close of his eighteen-month stay. He had reached Corinth early in 50 A.D., following the Jerusalem Conference.

Taking advantage of Gallio's recent arrival and lack of acquaintance with the situation, Jewish opponents preferred embarrassing charges against Paul. But Gallio, like Sergius Paulus was "a man of intelligence" (cf. Acts 13:7). Accordingly, he exonerated Paul of any sort of "wrongdoing," not even requiring that he answer charges so evidently spurious. In further exoneration of Christians and their leaders, Gallio watched with amusement while spectators thrashed Sosthenes, who had succeeded Crispus as "ruler of the synagogue."

Paul, of course, neither incited nor condoned the mistreatment of Sosthenes. That was a thoroughly pagan "turning of the tables." But Luke uses the story to illustrate how emphatically, by Roman ways, a Roman magistrate absolved the Church of slanderous charges.

An Interlude of Rest and Planning (Acts 18:22ff.). After leaving Corinth, Paul stopped briefly at Ephesus. This stop was preliminary to the fruition of his hopes on the third journey, when he worked there for nearly three years. Thence, he hurried to Jerusalem and then to Syrian Antioch.

At Antioch, Paul spent "some time." Restful fellowship and consultation with old friends prepared him for revisitation of churches in Phrygia and Galatia and the long-anticipated sojourn in Ephesus. Ephesus was to be the climax of Paul's career. Except for Alexandria and Rome, it was the empire's greatest city.

9

EPHESUS: A TREASURED DREAM COMES TRUE

ACTS 18:23 TO 19:41

Asia and Ephesus. The Greeks early discovered the value of western Asia Minor and colonized it. Persia later extended her empire westward and took control of the peninsula. Alexander broke Persia's hold on Greece and Asia, but his premature death left the latter to be the scene of wars for supremacy among his successors. The Romans came to restore order in 130 B.C. and organized Asia as a senatorial province. Under the peace Rome imposed, the region attained its maximum prosperity and prominence, the situation reflected in the New Testament.

Asia as a Roman province included the western half of Asia Minor. It was the first part of continental Asia known to the Romans and retained "Asia" as its name after Rome extended its authority far eastward. Climate, soil, geography, and Greek colonization combined to make the coastland province wealthy and influential. Only "Africa" among Roman provinces matched it in

prosperity and importance. By comparison with
Galatia, Macedonia, and Achaia, scenes of Paul's
earlier labors, Asia stood pre-eminent. It was as
though the Holy Spirit had saved the best for
last. Twice forbidden "by the Holy Spirit to
speak the word in Asia," at long last the apostle's
dream of an Asian ministry now came true.

A Veteran Promises to Return (Acts 18:18-21).
At the close of the second missionary journey,
Paul stopped briefly at Ephesus. There he left
Aquila and Priscilla to lay the groundwork for
his campaign in Asia. Under immediate neces-
sity to report to Jerusalem, Paul promised the
Ephesians, "I will return . . . if God wills." The
third missionary journey fulfilled that promise.

Ephesus originated as a colony of Athens and
during the period of Greek ascendancy held a
position of secondary importance. Under Macedonian and Roman rule it outdistanced Athens
culturally and economically. Only Smyrna, among
Asian cities, rivaled it, and Rome decided that
competition in favor of Ephesus by locating the
provincial capitol there and constituting it a
"Free City." Ordinarily proconsuls were attended
by six lictors, but such was the standing of
Ephesus that the proconsul there was attended
by twelve. No provincial capitol enjoyed closer
political ties with Rome.

The population of Ephesus was cosmopolitan

and its culture complex. Travelers between East and West, businessmen and religious pilgrims from all the world, Roman officials, and educators thronged the city and made it a sort of world in miniature. Roman order, Greek culture, sober Diaspora Judaism, and primitive superstitution existed side by side. All these stirred Paul's imagination and lured him to the scene of his greatest achievement and longest residence. Only Rome transcended Ephesus in challenge to the apostle. Acts appropriately makes the latter a stepping-stone to the world's capitol.

Artemis of the Ephesians (Acts 19:23-41). The temple of Artemis was one of the many attractions at Ephesus. It stood on the site of a shrine to an ancient nature goddess. The Greeks identified their own Artemis with that goddess and built a magnificent Greek temple for her worship. They did not, however, wholly succeed in altering the primitiveness of the practices of the ancient cult. Superstition, magic, and religiously sanctioned prostitution remained its accompaniments.

The temple was an important factor in the economy of Ephesus. Great wealth and profound emotional appeal made it in effect an "established church." That status is reflected in Acts and helps explain the city-wide disturbance when

Paul's preaching appeared to threaten its intrenched privileges.

Apollos and the Baptists (Acts 19:1-7). Apollos was an Alexandrian Jew, "well versed in the scriptures" and eloquent in their exposition. He came to Ephesus during the period between Paul's second and third missionary journeys. Subsequently he shifted his residence to Corinth, where he achieved a prominence comparable to that of Cephas and Paul (I Cor. 1:12).

According to Acts, Apollos "knew only the baptism of John." Yet it also represents him as having been "instructed in the way of the Lord." This could mean merely that he was an inadequately instructed Christian. More probably, it means that Apollos was a follower of John and came to Ephesus as a missionary for the sect kept alive by followers of John. The twelve disciples of John whom Paul rebaptized had probably become Baptists under Apollos' preaching (Acts 19:2-7). On this hypothesis, Aquila and Priscilla introduced him to the same spiritual experience that accompanied Paul's baptism of his Ephesian converts "in the name of the Lord Jesus" (Acts 19:5f.).

Apollos' recent activity as a missionary for a competing sect made it advisable that he shift the scene of his ministry from Ephesus to Corinth. Priscilla and Aquila assisted the transfer by writ-

ing the church at Corinth and urging his welcome there (Acts 18:27). Apollos' success at
Corinth may be inferred from his comparison
with Paul (I Cor. 1:12; 3:4-6; 4:6). His partisans
interpreted the relation as one of rivalry, but in
so doing they misunderstood the spirit of their
leader. He and Paul agreed that they were "fellow workmen for God" and that the church at
Corinth was "God's building" (I Cor. 3:9). When,
during Paul's stay at Ephesus, Apollos left Corinth, the apostle joined the Corinthians in urging
his return (I Cor. 16:12).

All the Residents of Asia (Acts 19:10). Paul
followed his usual pattern of preaching first in
Ephesian synagogues. When opposition developed, he withdrew and for two years used "the
hall of Tyrannus" and the residence of Aquila
and Priscilla as headquarters. But his was not a
localized ministry: "all the residents of Asia
heard the word of the Lord, both Jews and
Greeks."

Nearly a decade later, from a Roman prison,
the aging apostle, "an ambassador and now a
prisoner . . . for Christ Jesus," wrote letters to be
read to the churches at Laodicea and Colosse
(Col. 1:2; 2:1; 4:12-17; Philemon 2,9,23). These
churches owed their origin to Paul's initiative
during his stay at Ephesus. That Laodicea was
one of the seven churches addressed by the

prophet of Patmos suggests that all seven of those churches grew out of Paul's Asian ministry (Rev. 2:1 to 3:22).

Continuing Responsibility at Corinth (Acts 19:1; 20:1-6). Acts correlates Paul's relations with the churches at Corinth and Ephesus. Paul's own letters fill in the details. Nowhere else are Paul's strategy and untiring activity so clearly pictured.

The two epistles to Corinth incorporate the remains of at least four letters. They also reflect a two-sided interchange by messenger and letter. In First Corinthians 5:9 an earlier letter is mentioned and its subject stated. Similarly, in Second Corinthians 2:4 and 7:8 a letter, clearly not the one in which the allusions occur, is mentioned, the severity of which made the writer weep as he wrote and caused him "trouble and distress of mind" after he sent it. These data mean that Paul wrote Corinth four letters.

Nor was communication one-sided. By messenger and letter, Corinth kept in touch with Paul. Persons in Chloe's employ brought him news of factions (I Cor. 1:11f.). Leaders sought his counsel, listing their problems in a letter (I Cor. 7:1). Stephanos, Fortunatus, and Achaicus went to Ephesus for consultation (I Cor. 16:17). At different times, Paul sent Timothy and Titus to Corinth as trouble shooters (I Cor. 4:17; 16:10; II Cor. 7:6). In a particularly complicated situation, Paul himself went to Corinth, a visit unmentioned in Acts (II Cor. 12:14; 13:1).

Details are sufficiently abundant to make possible a reconstruction of the story. Early in his stay at Ephesus, Paul heard of the perplexity of Corinthians regarding their relations with pagan neighbors. For their guidance he wrote the letter mentioned in First Corinthians 5:9, a fragment of which is preserved in Second Corinthians 6:14 to 7:1. Chloe's employees, in Ephesus on business, brought news of emerging factions, and Timothy was sent to give counsel (I Cor. 1:11; 4:17). Hardly had Timothy started when an urgent letter requiring an immediate answer arrived from Corinth (I Cor. 7:1). Thereupon Paul wrote our First Corinthians and sent it in the hope it would reach Corinth before Timothy could arrive by way of Macedonia. Neither Timothy's visit nor Paul's letter pacified the situation. Accordingly, the apostle went in person to see what he could do (I Cor. 4:19-21; 11:34; 16:7). This visit resulted in repudiation by the church of its founder: he was publicly insulted, and left Corinth in humiliation. Deeply dejected, he was far from defeated. Relying on the memory and conscience of his erstwhile friends, he drafted and sent by Titus the severest letter he ever penned (II Cor. 2:1-5; 7:6-14; 12:14). The body of that letter is preserved in Second Corinthians 10 to 13. During the period suggested by Acts 20:2, Paul left Ephesus for Corinth by way of Macedonia. He took the roundabout way to allow his letter of severe reproof to take effect.

Probably at Philippi, Titus met him with news of penitence at Corinth and assurance of a cordial welcome awaiting him. Immediately Paul wrote a "kiss and make friends" letter, to be found in Second Corinthians 1 to 9 (excepting 6:14 to 7:1). That final letter he sent by Titus, while he and Macedonian friends followed at a more leisurely pace (II Cor. 9:4f.).

Ephesus in Early Christian Literature. Paul's four letters to Corinth inaugurated the prominence of Ephesus in Christian literature. It was destined to become the literary capital of the Church during the first two centuries. There, thirty years later, Paul's beloved Luke published his massive two-volume account of Christian beginnings, Luke-Acts. Stirred by the majestic picture of Paul in Acts, the erstwhile runaway slave Onesimus, now the venerable bishop of the church at Ephesus, saw the value of having Paul speak to Christendom through his letters (Ignatius *Ephesians* i.3; ii.1f.; vi.2). Using the account of Paul's journeys in Acts as a sort of road map, Onesimus retraced the apostle's steps and collected the remains of letters, until now in the keeping of the churches addressed. These letters he edited and published at Ephesus in about 95 A.D., giving them relevance for churches everywhere with a universalizing preface known in the New Testament as *The Epistle to the Ephesians*.

Within the same decade, and evidently influenced by Paul's recently published epistles, an Ephesian prophet named John published the book known as Revelation, prefacing it with letters to seven Asian churches. The published collection of Paul's letters contained epistles to seven churches, a coincidence which probably suggested the introduction of an Apocalypse with a corpus of letters to seven churches!

An unnamed Ephesian elder, more nearly of Paul's point of view than the prophet of Patmos, and the latter's contemporary, wrote the gospel and three epistles of John between 95 and 110 A.D., richly illustrating the fruitfulness of restating the gospel in terms of Hellenism. That a new intellectualism could be thus employed without compromising the truth earlier enshrined in Jewish forms of thought set a suggestive example and has supported freedom for interpreters of Christianity in succeeding centuries.

At Ephesus also, in about 125 A.D., and as a means of popularizing the Fourth Gospel, our four gospels were published under the general title, *The Gospel*, with the subtitles "According to Matthew," "According to Mark," "According to Luke," "According to John." There also, during the first half of the second century, the seven letters of Ignatius and Polycarp's great *Epistle to the Philippians* were treasured and preserved for posterity.

The Church has been in the publishing business ever since. By published books as well as by oral proclamation, evangelism and education have continued to disseminate the good news and establish the Church around the world.

10

THE LONG ROAD
TO ROME

ACTS 20:1 TO 28:31

Hastening to Jerusalem (Acts 20:1-38). "Near East Relief" is nothing new. It began in the neediness of ancient Palestine. Jews outside Palestine have always fared better than residents there. Diaspora Jews gave heavily to support their brethren in Judea as an aspect of religious duty. As Christianity became clearly distinguished from Judaism, Jewish Christians automatically lost their participation in Jewish charitable assistance.

Paul knew the system well, having been a Jew of the dispersion, from Tarsus in Cilicia. That knowledge inspired him repeatedly to raise money among his churches to assist Judean Christians. Fourteen years after his conversion, he accompanied Barnabas as joint bearer of funds contributed by the church at Antioch as "relief to the brethren who lived in Judea" (Acts 11:29; Gal. 2:10). Now, as the third missionary journey closes, Paul defers going to Rome and

Spain and hastens to Jerusalem to deliver a church-wide relief fund (Acts 20:16; Rom. 15:22-33).

But "relief" was only half of Paul's concern. A widening rift between Jewish and Gentile Christians threatened to "divide Christ up" (cf. I Cor. 1:12). Such division would make the Cross of Christ "seem an empty thing." Accordingly, having gathered funds among all Gentile churches, Paul determined to go with a committee from these churches to deliver and interpret the gift. Surely the bonds that made men one in Christ were more significant than worldly differences, including race.

Twofold concern with this collection explains the apostle's haste to reach Judea. That concern caused him to revisit Greece and Macedonia en route. Churches in both provinces were liberal contributors, and he wanted them represented in the committee (Acts 20:1-6; I Cor. 16:1-9; II Cor. 8:2-7; 9:1-5).

Romans: a By-product of Apostolic Haste (Acts 20:3; I Cor. 16:6). Paul spent the three winter months after leaving Ephesus at Corinth. He did more than raise money during those months. Under necessity to delay going to Rome and Spain, he wrote the greatest of his epistles to explain the delay and to prepare the Roman church to assist his plans.

Enlistment of Roman co-operation takes precedence over explanation of the delay. Paul needed Rome as a base of operations, as Antioch had served hitherto for his missionary journeys. That required appreciative understanding on the part of a church Paul had not founded and whose understanding of Christianity differed rather radically in some respects from his own. Controversy had dogged his steps and absorbed much of his energy in the East. At Antioch, and in Galatia, Macedonia, and Achaia, his major premise of the sufficiency of faith for approval by God had been challenged (Gal. 1 to 2; I Cor. 1:12,24; Phil. 3:2-11).

Such opposition might arise at Rome. To prevent it, Paul writes his greatest epistle, To the Romans. The epistle is not a compendium of the apostle's theology. Many of his themes are undeveloped there. Rather, it is an elaborate exposition of those aspects of his Christianity which had most frequently aroused opposition. Romans is therefore the fullest New Testament exposition of the meaning of "grace," the futility of legalism, the potency of faith, growth in actual Christlikeness, and the delineation of Christian character treasured by the early Church. The Cross is shown to be important as God's most effective instrument for arousing human faith. Faith is important because it is an assumption of the attitude of self-surrender and amenability on man's part that enables God to bestow his Holy Spirit. And the Holy Spirit is important as the means whereby man's moral frailty is remedied and his potential for growth in Christlikeness brought to fruition (Rom. 8:26-30; II Cor. 3:17-18). Salvation is thus the continuing growth in Christlikeness, and faith is man's original and necessary initiation of the process, which results in conformity to the image of God's Son. Sending that letter from Corinth, Paul, with a committee from the Gentile churches, hastens to Jerusalem.

The Cost of Prejudice (Acts 21:4-36). Having arrived at Jerusalem and been warmly welcomed by the Church, Paul went to extremes to avoid conflict with Jewish zealots (Acts 21:17-26). His efforts were of no avail. Mistaking fancy for fact, fanatics spread the rumor that the apostle had "brought Greeks into the temple and . . . defiled that holy place" (Acts 21:28). The resulting hysteria almost eventuated in a lynching. The Roman tribune "took soldiers and centurions" and rescued Paul lest religionists, their intelligence anesthetized by emotion, desecrate life to prevent desecration of architecture. Never again would the gospel's greatest missionary, and—save for his Lord—the world's greatest benefactor, be free from custody. Such is the cost of prejudice, then and now.

Jewish Condemnation and Roman Exoneration (*Acts 22:1 to 26:32*). Paul's defense before his Jewish accusers was astute, but futile. They listened to accounts of his Jewish upbringing, but became frenzied at the mention of his Gentile mission (Acts 22:1-21). Like Jonah of old, they could not believe God's love included all mankind.

Before the "chief priests and all the council," the distinguished prisoner fared little better than at the hands of the irresponsible street crowd: "like priest, like people." As always, when the blind lead the blind, "both fall into the pit" (Luke 6:39; Acts 22:30 to 24:21). Judaism's highest judicial tribunal shared the hysteria that made dispassionate investigation impossible.

By a vigorous espousal of the doctrine of resurrection, Paul briefly set Pharisee against Sadducee. But dissension ended the temporary respite and the tribune, fearing for Paul's life, again took him into protective custody, though according him the respect and rights due a Roman citizen.

As in the case of Jesus, conspiracy took precedence over justice under the pressure of irrational and tradition-bound religion. Paul had a married sister in Jerusalem, and her son brought him news that forty men, with the tacit approval of the chief priest, had vowed to kill him. This caused Claudius Lysias to transfer his prisoner to Caesarea for a hearing before Felix (Acts 23:26-35).

At the hands of Roman authorities, Paul fared well. Acts makes this emphatic. It explains the extended coverage of the three arraignments. Claudius Lysias, the arresting officer, gave the apostle the respect to which Roman citizenship entitled him. Nor did he ever appear against him in hearings before Felix, Festus, or Agrippa (Acts 21:32ff.; 22:25ff.; 23:26ff.). Not only so, but in his letter of transferal to Caesarea, Claudius Lysias expressed the opinion that the issues in the case were purely ecclesiastical and that the prisoner was "charged with nothing deserving of death or imprisonment under Roman law" (Acts 23:29; cf. 18:2ff.). Such reports of exoneration, repeated for Luke's generation, would have great value for the refutation of slanders current under Domitian.

Three Roman officials, two of them procurators and one a king, heard the charges and completely exonerated Paul. Felix, whose wife Drusilla was a Jewess, actually appears to have developed a liking for his prisoner and from time to time "sent for Paul and heard him speak on faith in Christ Jesus," being deeply stirred by his discussion of "justice and self-control and future judgment" (Acts 24:24ff.). Failure of Claudius to appear to press formal charges caused delay. That, coupled with the procurator's hope for money, left Paul a prisoner at Caesarea when Felix' term of office expired and Festus arrived to succeed him (Acts 24:27). Detention was thus to the discredit of the venal procurator, not the blameless apostle.

Festus listened at length to Jewish charges, first at Jerusalem and then at Caesarea. At a loss how to evaluate such sectarian complaints, he asked if Paul cared "to go to Jerusalem and be tried." With dignity that reflected courage and a clear conscience, the apostle replied: "I am standing before Caesar's tribunal, where I ought to be tried. . . . If I . . . have committed anything for which I deserve to die, I do not seek to escape death. . . . I appeal to Caesar" Festus granted the appeal and expressed the opinion privately to King Agrippa that the prisoner had done nothing under Roman law "deserving of death" (Acts 25:25).

Agrippa was the son of Herod Agrippa I, the personal friend of Caligula and Claudius. The older Agrippa had died in 44 A.D. while king of Judea (Acts 12:1-23). The younger Agrippa was only seventeen at the time, and Claudius kept him at his court in Rome. Eight years later, Herod, an uncle and king of Chalcis in Syria, died. Thereupon, Claudius appointed Agrippa, now twenty-five, to succeed his uncle. In 53 A.D., when Agrippa was thirty, Claudius gave him in exchange for Chalcis the kingship of northern Palestine. That appointment explains his presence at Caesarea (Acts 25:13ff.).

Bernice and Drusilla were the two daughters of Herod Agrippa I and sisters of the younger Agrippa, newly appointed King. Bernice had first married her uncle, the King of Chalcis. Then she had married Polemo, a Cilician official. She deserted Polemo because of her preference for her own brother, Agrippa, in whose company she came to Caesarea to visit Festus.

Festus discussed Paul's case with Agrippa because as Jews he and Bernice would be thoroughly familiar with Jewish tradition and theology. Having resided at the court of Claudius since his youth, Agrippa would also be familiar with Roman life and sympathies. In 66 A.D., Agrippa did his best to prevent the disastrous Jewish rebellion against Rome precipitated by the Zealot party. When the war came despite his efforts, Agrippa remained loyal to Rome. That loyalty to Rome was a matter of record fifteen years later when Luke wrote his account of Paul's hearing. It made Agrippa's exoneration of the apostle doubly significant for Roman provincial officials in Asia Minor during the reign of Domitian.

As in his defense before Felix, so now in presenting his case to Festus and Agrippa, Paul supplemented defense with positive proclamation of salvation through Christ and appealed persuasively to his judges to become Christians: so unashamed of the gospel he was (Acts 24:24ff.; 26:24ff.; Rom. 1:13ff.). Acts suggests near success in both cases. Though failing actually to convert his judges, the prisoner did establish his innocence, the joint verdict of Festus and Agrippa being: "This man is doing nothing to deserve death or imprisonment" and but for his appeal to Caesar "could have been set free" (Acts 26:31f.).

Divine Denouement: Arrival at Rome (Acts 28). Paul knew and proclaimed "the depth of the riches and wisdom . . . of God" and the inscrutability of "his ways" (Rom. 11:33). He had long desired to visit Rome and was sure that in his own time and way God would make the visit possible (Rom. 1:10). Now, despite his status as a prisoner and the chains that emphasized that status, he regards himself nonetheless Christ's "ambassador," who by his suffering completed what might be lacking "in the sufferings of Christ" (Col. 1:24; Philemon 9, both written from Roman imprisonment).

Acts bears out the point of view expressed in the apostle's imprisonment letters. He, like his

Lord, is more than the victim of human conspiracy. Through him God is working in his own
mysterious ways for the salvation of a lost world.
Paul appears more nearly as a distinguished
guest than as a prisoner. He is at Rome "on business for his King" and he preaches with freedom
to all within the range of his voice "openly and
unhindered" (Acts 28:31). So Luke closes his
story.

No account of a trial at Rome is given. Had
Paul been exonerated and released, it would
surely have been reported. That he and Peter
died as victims of Nero's attack on the Church
is too deeply a part of Christian tradition to lack
some basis in fact. The silence of Acts is best
explained on the ground that report of an adverse decision at Rome would have been disastrous for the Christian cause in Asia Minor.

The most fruitful permanent outcome of Paul's
two years at Rome, of course, was the letters he
wrote to Asian and Macedonian churches, Colossians, Philemon, Philippians. But for Luke arrival
at Rome was the divine denouement. Anything
added would have been an anticlimax. What
mattered for the support of the faith of third-
generation Christians and for the conversion of
hesitant listeners, "the almost persuaded," was
that an overarching providence had superin-
tended the triumphant march of the gospel from

Jerusalem to Rome. This had made possible the establishment of churches in the principal cities of the Empire. In them all and to earth's end, Christ now had witnesses, courageous and unashamed.

SUGGESTED
BIBLIOGRAPHY

Barclay, William, *The Acts of the Apostles*. Philadelphia: The Westminster Press, 1957.

Barnett, Albert E., *The New Testament: Its Making and Meaning*. New York: Abingdon Press, 1958.
The Church: Its Origin and Task. Nashville: National Methodist Student Movement, 1960.

Cadbury, Henry J., *The Style and Literary Method of Luke*. Cambridge: Harvard University Press, 1920.
The Making of Luke-Acts. New York: The Macmillan Co., 1927.
"Acts of the Apostles," in *The Beginnings of Christianity*, edited by F. J. Foakes-Jackson and Kirsopp Lake, Vol. V. London: The Macmillan Co., 1933.
The Book of Acts in History. New York: Harper & Bros., 1955.

Craig, Clarence Tucker, *The Beginning of Christianity*. New York: Abingdon Press, 1943.

Foakes-Jackson, F. J., *The Acts of the Apostles*, in Moffatt New Testament Commentaries. New York: Harper & Bros., 1931.

Goguel, Maurice, *The Birth of Christianity*, translated by H. C. Snape. New York: The Macmillan Co., 1954.

Knox, John, *Philemon Among the Letters of Paul*. New York: Abingdon Press, 1959.

Lietzmann, Hans, *The Beginnings of the Christian Church*, translated by Bertram Lee Woolf. New York: Chas. Scribner's Sons, 1937.

Luccock, Halford E., *Acts of the Apostles in Present-day Preaching*. Chicago: Willett, Clark & Co., 1939.

Macgregor, G. H. C., "The Acts of the Apostles," in *The Interpreter's Bible*, Vol. 9. New York: Abingdon Press, 1954.

Rackham, Richard B., *The Acts of the Apostles*. Westminster Commentaries. London: Methuen & Co., 1912.

Scott, Ernest Findlay, *The Nature of the Early Church*, New York: Chas. Scribner's Sons, 1941.

Each 50 cents unless otherwise marked

[4]

Discover all of these

REFLECTION BOOKS

Each 50 cents unless otherwise marked

[4]